EVOLVE

STUDENT'S BOOK
with Digital Pack

Leslie Anne Hendra, Mark Ibbotson,
and Kathryn O'Dell

T0372779

1B

CAMBRIDGE
UNIVERSITY PRESS

Shaftesbury Road, Cambridge CB2 8EA, United Kingdom

One Liberty Plaza, 20th Floor, New York, NY 10006, USA

477 Williamstown Road, Port Melbourne, VIC 3207, Australia

314–321, 3rd Floor, Plot 3, Splendor Forum, Jasola District Centre, New Delhi – 110025, India

103 Penang Road, #05-06/07, Visioncrest Commercial, Singapore 238467

Cambridge University Press & Assessment is a department of the University of Cambridge.

We share the University's mission to contribute to society through the pursuit of education, learning and research at the highest international levels of excellence.

www.cambridge.org
Information on this title: www.cambridge.org/9781009231787

First published with Digital Pack 2022

20 19 18 17 16 15 14 13 12 11

Printed in Malaysia by Vivar Printing

A catalogue record for this publication is available from the British Library

ISBN 978-1-009-23167-1 Student's Book with eBook
ISBN 978-1-009-23176-3 Student's Book with Digital Pack
ISBN 978-1-009-23177-0 Student's Book with Digital Pack A
ISBN 978-1-009-23178-7 Student's Book with Digital Pack B
ISBN 978-1-108-40894-3 Workbook with Audio
ISBN 978-1-108-40859-2 Workbook with Audio A
ISBN 978-1-108-41191-2 Workbook with Audio B
ISBN 978-1-108-40512-6 Teacher's Edition with Test Generator
ISBN 978-1-108-41062-5 Presentation Plus
ISBN 978-1-108-41201-8 Class Audio CDs
ISBN 978-1-108-40791-5 Video Resource Book with DVD
ISBN 978-1-009-23149-7 Full Contact with Digital Pack

Additional resources for this publication at www.cambridge.org/evolve

ACKNOWLEDGMENTS

The *Evolve* publishers would like to thank the following individuals and institutions who have contributed their time and insights into the development of the course:

Ivanova Monteros A., **Universidad Tecnológica Equinoccial (UTE)**, Ecuador; Monica Frenzel, **Universidad Andrés Bello**, Chile; Antonio Machuca Montalvo, **Organización The Institute TITUELS**, **Veracruz**, Mexico; Daniel Martin, **CELLEP**, Brazil; Roberta Freitas, **IBEU**, Brazil; Verónica Nolivos Arellano, Language Coordinator, Quito, Ecuador; Daniel Lowe, **Lowe English Services**, Panama; Maria Araceli Hernández Tovar, **Instituto Tecnológico Superior de San Luis Potosí**, Capital, Mexico; Lenise Butler, **Laureate**, Mexico; Gloria González Meza, **Instituto Politecnico Nacional, ESCA (University)**, Mexico; Miguel Ángel López, **Universidad Europea de Madrid**, Spain; Diego Ribeiro Santos, **Universidade Anhembi Morumbi**, São Paulo, Brazil; Esther Carolina Euceda Garcia, **UNITEC (Universidad Tecnologica Centroamericana)**, Honduras.

To our student cast, who have contributed their ideas and their time, and who appear throughout this book:

Anderson Batista, Brazil; Carolina Nascimento Negrão, Brazil; Felipe Martinez Lopez, Mexico; Jee-Hyo Moon, South Korea ; Jinny Lara, Honduras; Josue Lozano, Honduras; Julieth C. Moreno Delgado, Colombia; Larissa Castro, Honduras.

And special thanks to Katy Simpson, teacher and writer at *myenglishvoice.com*; and Raquel Ribeiro dos Santos, EFL teacher, EdTech researcher, blogger, and lecturer.

Authors' Acknowledgments:

The authors would like to extend their warmest thanks to all of the team at Cambridge University Press who were involved in creating this course. In particular, they would like to thank Ruby Davies and Robert Williams for their kindness, enthusiasm, and encouragement throughout the writing of the A1 level. They would also like to express their appreciation to Caroline Thiriau, whose understanding and support have been of great value. And they would like to thank Katie La Storia for her dedication and enthusiasm throughout the project.

Kathryn O'Dell would like to thank her parents (and grandparents) for passing down a love for words and stories. She also thanks her husband, Kevin Hurdman, for his loving support.

Leslie Anne Hendra would like to thank Michael Stuart Clark, her *sine qua non*, for his support and encouragement during this and other projects.

Mark Ibbotson would like to thank Aimy and Tom for their patience and understanding as family life was bent and squeezed around the project, and – especially – Nathalie, whose energy and creative solutions made it all possible.

The authors and publishers acknowledge the following sources of copyright material and are grateful for the permissions granted. While every effort has been made, it has not always been possible to identify the sources of all the material used, or to trace all copyright holders. If any omissions are brought to our notice, we will be happy to include the appropriate acknowledgements on reprinting and in the next update to the digital edition, as applicable.

Photo:

Key: B = Below, BG = Background, BL = Below Left, BR = Below Right, C = Centre, CL = Centre Left, CR = Centre Right, L = Left, R = Right, TC = Top Centre, TL = Top Left, TR = Top Right.

All images are sourced from Getty Images.

p. xvi (listen): Tara Moore/DigitalVision; p. xvi (say): Tara Moore/The Image Bank; p. xvi (write): Kohei Hara/DigitalVision; p. xvi (watch): Felbert+Eickenberg/Stock4B; p. xvi (students), p. 124: Klaus Vedfelt/DigitalVision; p. 106 (C): Hero Images; p. 66 (photo 5), p. 68 (2d, 2f, 2i), p. 82 (TC), p. 88, p. 117, p. 120 (fish), p. xvi (read): Westend61; p. 74: Caiaimage/Sam Edwards; p. 98 (walk): Alistair Berg/DigitalVision; p. 74, 84, 94, 106, 116, 126: Tom Merton/Caiaimage; p. 80, p. 114 (woman): Tetra Images; p. 84 (soccer): Hinterhaus Productions/DigitalVision; p. 108 (book): PeopleImages/DigitalVision; p.66 (photo 2), p. 72 (cat), p. 118 (bread): Dorling Kindersley; p. 72 (cat), p. 118 (tomato): Dave King/Dorling Kindersleyl; p. 65: jameslee999/Vetta; p. 66 (photo 1): Phil Boorman/The Image Bank; p. 66 (photo 3): Vincent Besnault/The Image Bank; p. 66 (photo 4): David Zach/Stone; p. 66 (photo 6): LM Productions/Photodisc; p. 67: Jonathan Knowles/The Image Bank; p. 68 (2a, 2b): alvarez/E+; p. 68 (2c): Samuelsson, Kristofer; p. 68 (2e): Plume Creative/DigitalVision; p. 68 (2g):

Jordan Siemens/Taxi; p. 68 (2h): Ezra Bailey/Taxi; p. 69: Lorentz Gullachsen/The Image Bank; p. 70 (BL): Robert Kneschke/EyeEm; p. 70 (BG), p. 108 (beautiful): Dougal Waters/DigitalVision; p. 71: Flavio Edreira/EyeEm; p. 72: Lane Oatey/Blue Jean Images; p. 73: Dave Nagel/Taxi; p. 75: Mint Images RF; p. 76 (surf): Christian Kober/AWL Images; p. 76 (skateboard): yanik88/iStock/Getty Images Plus; p. 76 (snowboarding): Maximilian Groß/EyeEm; p. 76 (draw): Ruth Jenkinson/Dorling Kindersley; p. 76 (boys): Resolution Productions/Blend Images; p. 76 (paint): Glowimages; p. 76 (sing): Kyle Monk/Blend Images; p. 76 9(dance): catalinere/iStock/Getty Images Plus; p. 76 (guitar): Justin Case/Taxi; p. 76 (swim): pixdeluxe/E+; p. 76 (wheel): Philip Gatward/Dorling Kindersley; p. 76 (CR), p. 121: Jose Luis Pelaez Inc/Blend Images; p. 77: Lilly Roadstones/The Image Bank; p. 78: Reza Estakhrian/Iconica; p. 79: PeopleImages/E+; p. 81: Allison Michael Orenstein/The Image Bank; p. 82 (TL): Kristy-Anne Glubish; p. 82 (TR): PhonlamaiPhoto/iStock/Getty Images Plus; p. 84 (photo 1): ibrahimaslann/iStock Editorial/Getty Images Plus; p. 84 (photo 2): Marc Romanelli/Blend Images; p. 84 (photo 3): Yew! Images/Image Source; p. 84 (photo 4): PaulBiryukov/iStock/Getty Images Plus; p. 85: Johannes Spahn/EyeEm; p. 86 (airplane): Jan Stromme/The Image Bank; p. 86 (woman): Caroline Schiff/Taxi; p. 86 (girl): Peathegee Inc/Blend Images; p. 86 (country): Instants/E+; p. 86 (parrot): Busakorn Pongparnit/Moment; p. 86 (boat): Richard Cummins/Lonely Planet Images; p. 86 (park): Lidija Kamansky/Moment Open; p. 87 (C): Waring Abbott/Michael Ochs Archives; p. 87 (hikers): Debra Brash/Perspectives; p. 87 (Lake): Jeff Greenberg/Universal Images Group; p. 89: Cláudio Policarpo/EyeEm; p. 90: Image Source; p. 92: Anna Gorin/Moment; p. 93: hadynyah/E+; p. 94 (Jim): John Lund/Marc Romanelli/Blend Images; p. 93 (Flo): Blend Images - Erik Isakson/Brand X Pictures; p. 94 (Carter): Alexander Robinson/Blend Images; p. 97: Darryl Leniuk/DigitalVision; p. 98 (TL): Chan Srithaweeporn/Moment; p. 98 (art): Randy Faris/Corbis/VCG; p. 98 (dinner, shopping): Cultura RM Exclusive/Frank and Helena; p. 98 (airport): Maskot; p. 98 (picnic): Uwe Krejci/DigitalVision; p. 99: Billy Hustace/Corbis Documentary; p. 100 (fall): Shobeir Ansari/Moment; p. 100 (summer): AL Hedderly/Moment; p. 100 (spring): Lelia Valduga; p. 100 (rainy): Chalabala/iStock/Getty Images Plus; p. 100 (dry): skodonnell/E+; p. 101: Julia Davila-Lampe/Moment; p. 102: Caiaimage/Chris Ryan; p. 103: filadendron/E+; p. 104: Rudimencial/iStock/Getty Images Plus; p. 105: ©Leonardo Muniz/Moment; 106 (TL): Toshi Sasaki/Photodisc; p. 106 (TC): skynesher/iStock/Getty Images Plus; p. 106 (TR): AJ_Watt/E+; p. 106 (CL): Luke Stettner/Photonica; p. 106 (CR): Mike Kemp/Blend Images; p. 107: Shanina/iStock/Getty Images Plus; p. 107 (TR): Simon Winnall/Taxi; p. 108 (kart): Images Of Our Lives/Archive Photos; p.108 (awful): PM Images/Stone; p. 108 (dog): Kevin Kozicki/Image Source; p. 108 (baby, quiet baby): Emma Kim/Cultura; p. 108 (fast car): Martin Barraud/Caiaimage; p. 108 (slow car): Michael Mrozek/EyeEm; p. 108 (shoe): Jeffrey Coolidge/The Image Bank; p. 108 (vacation): swissmediavision/E+; p. 109: Satoshi Yamada/EyeEm; p. 110: NexTser/iStock/Getty Images Plus; p. 111: real444/E+; p. 112: Mark Cuthbert/UK Press; p. 113: Mike Powell/Stone; p. 114 (toy car): Peter Zander/Photolibrary; p. 114 (shoe): Willer Amorim/EyeEm; 114 (comic): Bernd Vogel/Corbis; p. 115: George Steinmetz/Corbis Documentary; p. 116: Shan Shui/DigitalVision; p. 118 (chicken): Floortje/E+; p. 118 (coconut): RedHelga/E+; p. 118 (pineapple): Moodboard Stock Photography Ltd./Canopy; p. 118 (apple): t_kimura/E+; p. 118 (soup): David Marsden/Photolibrary; p. 118 (butter): SvetlanaK/iStock/Getty Images Plus; p. 118 (banana): Andy Crawford/Dorling Kindersley; p. 118 (cheese): Steven Mark Needham/Corbis Documentary; p. 118 (potato): jerryhat/E+; p. 114 (beef): Frank Bean/UpperCut Images; p. 118 (sandwich), p. 125: LauriPatterson/E+; p. 118 (orange): julichka/E+; p. 118 (lamb): pmphoto/iStock/Getty Images Plus; p. 118 (crackers): Bernard Prost/StockFood Creative; p. 118 (CR): Stephanie Leong/EyeEm; p. 119: Lumina Images/Blend Images; p. 120 (steak): Joy Skipper/Photolibrary; p. 120 (pizza): Nomadsoul1/iStock/Getty Images Plus; p. 120 (beans): Angela Bragato/EyeEm; p. 120 (chocolate): Angela Bragato/EyeEm; p. 120 (cookies): DigiPub/Moment; p. 120 (water): Retno Ayu Adiati/EyeEm; p. 122: Justin Case/The Image Bank; p. 123: Maarten De Beer/EyeEm; p.124 (Chinese): Naltik/iStock/Getty Images Plus; p. 124 (Mexican): rez-art/iStock/Getty Images Plus; p. 124 (Italian): Jon Spaull/Perspectives; p. 126: andresr/E+.

The following images are sourced from other libraries:

p. 76 (music): otnaydur/Shutterstock; p. 84 (CR): AlanHaynes.com/Alamy Stock Photo.

Front cover photography by Arctic-Images/The Image Bank/Getty Images.

Illustrations by: Joanna Kerr (New Division) p. 100; Dusan Lakicevic (Beehive Illustration) pp. 88, 90, 91.

Audio production by CityVox, New York.

EVOLVE

SPEAKING MATTERS

EVOLVE is a six-level American English course for adults and young adults, taking students from beginner to advanced levels (CEFR A1 to C1).

Drawing on insights from language teaching experts and real students, EVOLVE is a general English course that gets students speaking with confidence.

This student-centered course covers all skills and focuses on the most effective and efficient ways to make progress in English.

Confidence in teaching.
Joy in learning.

Better Learning WITH EVOLVE

Better Learning is our simple approach where insights we've gained from research have helped shape content that drives results. Language evolves, and so does the way we learn. This course takes a flexible, student-centered approach to English language teaching.

CAMBRIDGE

EVOLVE

STUDENT'S BOOK

Leslie Anne Hendra, Mark Ibbotson, and Kathryn O'Dell

1

Experience Better Learning

Meet our student contributors

Videos and ideas from real students feature throughout the Student's Book.

Our student contributors describe themselves in three words.

LARISSA CASTRO

Friendly, honest, happy
Centro Universitario
Tecnológico, Honduras

JINNY LARA

Free your mind
Centro Universitario
Tecnológico, Honduras

CAROLINA NASCIMENTO NEGRÃO

Nice, determined, hard-working
Universidade Anhembi Morumbi,
Brazil

JOSUE LOZANO

Enthusiastic, cheerful, decisive
Centro Universitario
Tecnológico, Honduras

JULIETH C. MORENO DELGADO

Decisive, reliable, creative
Fundación Universitaria
Monserrate, Colombia

ANDERSON BATISTA

Resilient, happy, dreamer
Universidade Anhembi
Morumbi, Brazil

FELIPE MARTINEZ LOPEZ

Reliable, intrepid, sensitive
Universidad del Valle de
México, Mexico

JEE-HYO MOON (JUNE)

Organized, passionate, diligent
Mission College, USA

Student-generated content

EVOLVE is the first course of its kind to feature real student-generated content.
We spoke to over 2,000 students from all over the world about the topics they
would like to discuss in English and in what situations they would like to be able
to speak more confidently.

The ideas are included throughout the Student's Book and the students appear
in short videos responding to discussion questions.

INSIGHT

Research shows that
achievable speaking role
models can be a powerful
motivator.

CONTENT

Bite-sized videos feature
students talking about
topics in the Student's
Book.

RESULT

Students are motivated
to speak and share their
ideas.

"It's important to provide learners with interesting or stimulating topics."

Teacher, Mexico (Global Teacher Survey, 2017)

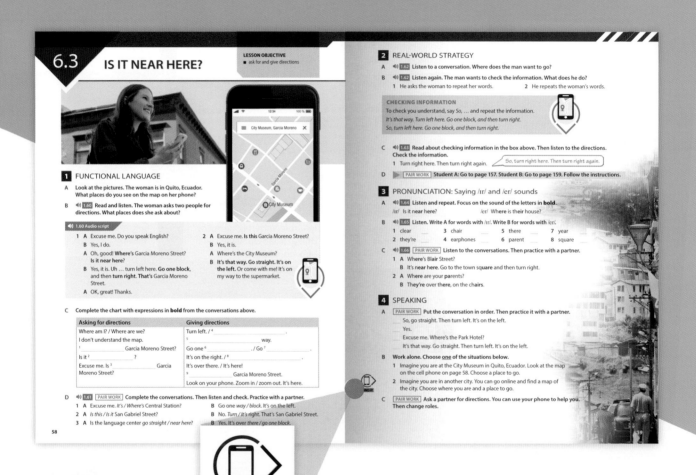

Find it

FIND IT

INSIGHT

Research with hundreds of teachers and students across the globe revealed a desire to expand the classroom and bring the real world in.

CONTENT

Find it are smartphone activities that allow students to bring live content into the class and personalize the learning experience with research and group activities.

RESULT

Students engage in the lesson because it is meaningful to them.

Designed for success

Pronunciation

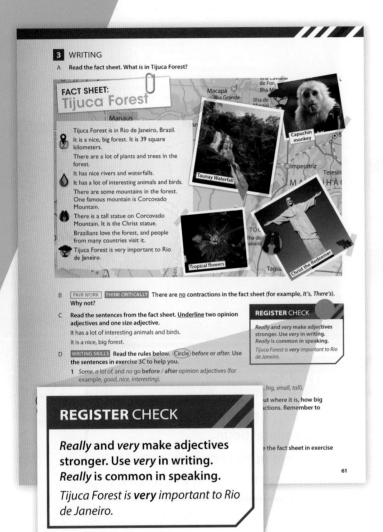

INSIGHT

Research shows that only certain aspects of pronunciation actually affect comprehensibility and inhibit communication.

CONTENT

EVOLVE focuses on the aspects of pronunciation that most affect communication.

RESULT

Students understand more when listening and can be clearly understood when they speak.

Register check

INSIGHT

Teachers report that their students often struggle to master the differences between written and spoken English.

CONTENT

Register check draws on research into the Cambridge English Corpus and highlights potential problem areas for learners.

RESULT

Students transition confidently between written and spoken English and recognize different levels of formality as well as when to use them appropriately.

GOOD PLACES

LESSON OBJECTIVE
■ talk about places in the city

1 LANGUAGE IN CONTEXT

A 🔊 1.57 Lucas and Robert are in New York City. Read and listen to their conversation. Where is Lucas from? Where is Robert from? What does Lucas want to do on Saturday?

B 🔊 1.57 Read and listen again. Are the sentences true or false?
1 Lucas has a lot of time in New York City.
2 There is no restaurant in the hotel.

🔊 1.57 Audio script

GLOSSARY
neighborhood (n) an area of a city

Lucas I'm here, in New York City, for a week. And then I go home to Paris on Sunday.	
Robert So you don't have a lot of time to see my great city.	**Lucas** Cool! What about places to eat? There's no **restaurant** in my hotel.
Lucas No, I don't. There's no free time this week – it's work, work, work! But I have some time on Saturday.	**Robert** Hmm … for breakfast, there's a nice **café** near here. And there are a lot of great restaurants in this neighborhood, too.
Robert OK. There are a lot of places to see and things to do on the weekend. Where is your **hotel**?	**Lucas** Great. Do you know some good **stores**? I don't have a lot of free time, but …
Lucas It's near Central Park.	**Robert** Oh, yeah. There are a lot of great stores in New York. So … no museum, no park, no zoo – just shopping?
Robert No way! Central Park is great. There are some interesting museums near the **park**. Oh, and there's a **zoo** in the park!	**Lucas** Yes!

INSIDER ENGLISH

Use *No way!* to show surprise.
No way! Central Park is great.

2 VOCABULARY: Places in cities

A 🔊 1.58 Listen and repeat the words.

bookstore hospital movie theater restaurant supermarket
café hotel museum school zoo
college mall park store

B ▶ Now do the vocabulary exercises for 6.1 on page 145.

C PAIR WORK Which three places in cities do you both like? Which three don't you like?

54

3 GRAMMAR: There's, There are; a lot of, some, no

A Circle the correct answers. Use the sentences in the grammar box to help you.
1 Use *There's* with singular / plural nouns.
2 Use *There are* with singular / plural nouns.
3 Use *an / no* in negative sentences.
4 Use *some* for exact numbers / when you don't know how many things there are.

There's (= There is), There are; a lot of, some, no

There's no free time this week.	There are some interesting museums near the park.	no = zero
There's a zoo in the park.		a/an = one
There's a nice café near here.	There are a lot of good places to see on the weekend.	some = a small number
		a lot of = a large number

B Circle the correct words to complete the sentences.
1 There's / There are a lot of stores in the mall.
2 There's / There are a supermarket near the college.
3 There are a / some good cafés on Boston Road.
4 There's a / a lot of big hospital in the city.
5 There are a lot of / no stores, so it's great for shopping.
6 In my city, there are a / no zoos.

C ▶ Now go to page 134. Look at the grammar chart and do the grammar exercise for 6.1.

D Write sentences about your city. Use *there is/there are, a/an, some, a lot of,* and *no*. Then check your accuracy.

There's _____ .
There's _____ .
There are _____ .
There are _____ .
There is/are no _____ .

✓ **ACCURACY** CHECK

Use *there are*, **not** *there is*, before *a lot of* and *some* + plural noun.
There is some museums in this city. ✗
There are some museums in this city. ✓

E PAIR WORK Compare your sentences with a partner.

4 SPEAKING

PAIR WORK Talk about the things in your neighborhood. Then compare with a partner. What's the same? What's different?

There are some good restaurants near my home.

Same! And there's a movie theater near my home.

55

✓ **ACCURACY** CHECK

Use *there are*, **not** *there is*, before *a lot of* and *some* + plural noun.

There is some museums in this city. ✗
There are some museums in this city. ✓

Accuracy check

INSIGHT

Some common errors can become fossilized if not addressed early on in the learning process.

CONTENT

Accuracy check highlights common learner errors (based on unique research into the Cambridge Learner Corpus) and can be used for self-editing.

RESULT

Students avoid common errors in their written and spoken English.

"The presentation is very clear and there are plenty of opportunities for student practice and production."

Jason Williams, Teacher, Notre Dame Seishin University, Japan

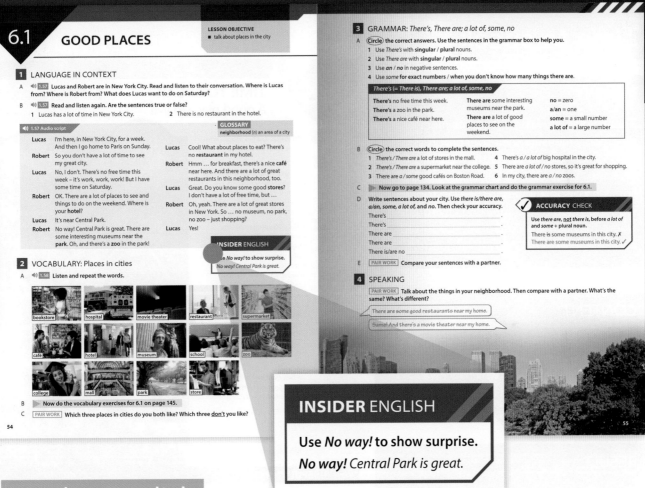

Insider English

INSIGHT

Even in a short exchange, idiomatic language can inhibit understanding.

CONTENT

Insider English focuses on the informal language and colloquial expressions frequently found in everyday situations.

RESULT

Students are confident in the real world.

You spoke. We listened.

Students told us that speaking is the most important skill for them to master, while teachers told us that finding speaking activities which engage their students and work in the classroom can be challenging.

That's why EVOLVE has a whole lesson dedicated to speaking: Lesson 5, *Time to speak.*

Time to speak

INSIGHT

Speaking ability is how students most commonly measure their own progress, but is also the area where they feel most insecure. To be able to fully exploit speaking opportunities in the classroom, students need a safe speaking environment where they can feel confident, supported, and able to experiment with language.

CONTENT

Time to Speak is a unique lesson dedicated to developing speaking skills and is based around immersive tasks which involve information sharing and decision making.

RESULT

Time to speak lessons create a buzz in the classroom where speaking can really thrive, evolve, and take off, resulting in more confident speakers of English.

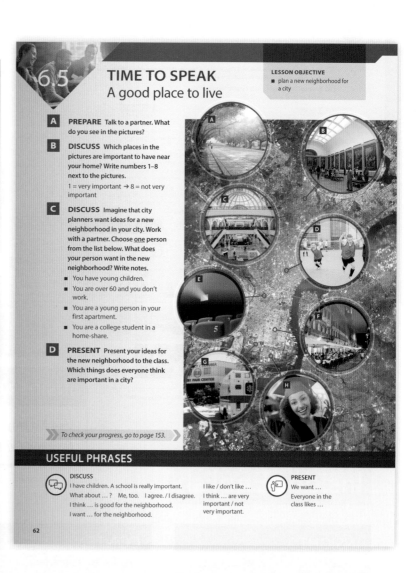

Experience Better Learning with EVOLVE: a course that helps both teachers and students on every step of the language learning journey.

Speaking matters. Find out more about creating safe speaking environments in the classroom.

EVOLVE unit structure

Unit opening page

Each unit opening page activates prior knowledge and vocabulary and immediately gets students speaking.

Lessons 1 and 2

These lessons present and practice the unit vocabulary and grammar in context, helping students discover language rules for themselves. Students then have the opportunity to use this language in well-scaffolded, personalized speaking tasks.

Lesson 3

This lesson is built around a functional language dialogue that models and contextualizes useful fixed expressions for managing a particular situation. This is a real world strategy to help students handle unexpected conversational turns.

Lesson 4

This is a combined skills lesson based around an engaging reading or listening text. Each lesson asks students to think critically and ends with a practical writing task.

Lesson 5

Time to speak is an entire lesson dedicated to developing speaking skills. Students work on collaborative, immersive tasks which involve information sharing and decision making.

CONTENTS

Functional language	Listening	Reading	Writing	Speaking
■ Answer the phone and greet people; ask how things are going **Real-world strategy** ■ React to news		**Jamie's blog** ■ A blog about a difficult place	**A blog post** ■ A blog about a busy place ■ *and, also,* and *too*	■ Talk about the lives of people in a picture ■ Talk about good and bad times to call someone ■ Tell a friend what you are doing right now ■ Talk about your news **Time to speak** ■ Talk about your life these days
■ Ask for and give for opinions **Real-world strategy** ■ Explain and say more about an idea	**Technology Talks** ■ A podcast about computers		**A comment** ■ Comments about an online post ■ Quotations	■ Discuss activities you do ■ Talk about skills you have ■ Talk about what you can and can't do at work ■ Ask and answer questions in a job interview **Time to speak** ■ Discuss national skills
■ Ask for and give information **Real-world strategy** ■ Ask someone to repeat something		**Places to go near Puno** ■ A travel guide	**A description** ■ A description of a place ■ Imperatives to give advice	■ Talk about a place you like ■ Describe people and places in a picture ■ Talk about organizing a trip ■ Ask for information at an airport store **Time to speak** ■ Talk about planning a vacation
■ Make, accept, and refuse suggestions **Real-world strategy** ■ Say why you can't do something	**Montevideo** ■ A TV travel show		**An invitation** ■ An event invitation ■ Contractions	■ Talk about your plans for the future ■ Talk about outdoor activities in your city ■ Talk about clothes to take for a trip ■ Talk about where to go out for dinner **Time to speak** ■ Plan a fun weekend in your home city
■ Express uncertainty **Real-world strategy** ■ Take time to think		**Picturing memories** ■ An article about things people keep	**An email** ■ An email to a friend ■ Paragraphs and topic sentences	■ Describe a happy time in your life ■ Talk about things you remember ■ Talk about colors you remember from when you were a child ■ Talk about people in a movie **Time to speak** ■ Present your memories of a TV show from your past
■ Offer, request and accept food and drink **Real-world strategy** ■ Use *so* and *really* to make words stronger	**Where do you want to eat?** ■ A conversation about restaurants on a food app		**A review** ■ A restaurant review ■ Commas in lists	■ Describe a good meal you had ■ Talk about snacks and small meals you like ■ Talk about a meal you had in a restaurant ■ Ask for food in a restaurant or at a friend's house **Time to speak** ■ Design a menu for a new restaurant

CLASSROOM LANGUAGE

◀)) **1.02** **Get started**
Hi. / Hello.
What's your name?
My name is _____.
This is my class.
This is my partner.
This is my teacher.

Ask for help
I don't understand.
I have a question.
How do you say _____
in English?
What does _____ mean?
How do you spell _____?
Can you repeat that, please?
Sorry, what page?

Your teacher
I'm your teacher.
Open your book.
Close your book.
Go to page _____.
Do you have any questions?

Listen.

Say.

Read.

Write.

Watch.

Work in pairs.

Work in groups.

- talk about activities around the house
- ask and answer questions about travel
- share news on the phone
- write a blog about things happening now
- ask what people are doing these days

NOW IS GOOD

7

START SPEAKING

A **Say what you see in the picture. Who are the people? Are they at work or do they have free time? Where are they?**

B **Are they busy now? Do they have a busy life?**

C **Talk about things:**
- they do *and* you do.
- you do, but they don't.
- they do, but you don't.

7.1 A GOOD TIME TO CALL

LESSON OBJECTIVE
■ talk about activities around the house

1 LANGUAGE IN CONTEXT

A 🔊 **2.02** David calls his sister Ariana on the phone. Read and listen. (Circle) the correct answers.

1 Ariana is *the mother / the daughter*.

2 Jason is *Ariana's son / Ariana's husband*.

3 Stevie is *Ariana's son / Ariana's daughter*.

4 Julia is *Ariana's sister / Stevie's sister*.

🔊 **2.02 Audio script**

David   Hi, Ariana. It's David. Are you busy? Is this a good time to call?

Ariana Um, well, I'm **cooking** breakfast right now, and Jason's **helping** the children— Jason, Stevie isn't drinking his milk.

David   Oh, yeah. It's a school day today.

Ariana That's right, so …

David   What time do they leave for school?

Ariana Usually at 8:00, but we're running late today — Jason, give this to the kids, OK? Thanks. — OK, David, they're eating breakfast now.

David   Do they like their classes?

Ariana Yes, and they're learning a lot — Julia, you're not eating. Please eat your breakfast now! — Sorry, David. This isn't a good time to talk.

B 🔊 **2.02** Read and listen again. Is David busy now? Why does Ariana say "*This isn't a good time to talk.*"?

GLOSSARY
kids (*n*) children (informal)
running late (*phrase*) you are late

2 VOCABULARY: Activities around the house

A 🔊 **2.03** Look at the pictures. Listen and repeat.

1 I'm cleaning the kitchen.

2 I'm cooking dinner.

3 I'm washing my hair.

4 I'm brushing my teeth.

5 I'm doing the dishes.

6 I'm helping my daughters. They're taking a bath.

B Add the words in the box to the verbs.

breakfast	the dog	my hair	my homework	~~my room~~	a shower

1 **clean** the kitchen / ____my room____

2 **cook** dinner / _____

3 **wash** my hair / _____

4 **brush** my teeth / _____

5 **take** a bath / _____

6 **do** the dishes / _____

C ▶ Now do the vocabulary exercises for 7.1 on page 146.

D PAIR WORK Do you do your homework <u>and</u> talk on the phone? What other activities do you do at the same time? For ideas, watch June's video.

REAL STUDENT
Do you do the things June does?

3 GRAMMAR: Present continuous statements

A (Circle) the correct answer. Use the sentences in the grammar box to help you.

1 Use the present continuous to talk about **things happening right now or around now / finished things**.

2 Sentences 1, 2, and 3 in the grammar box are about **right now / around now**.

3 Sentence 4 is about **right now / around now**.

4 To make the present continuous, use *am/is/are* and a **verb + -ing / verb + -s**.

Present continuous statements

1 **I'm cooking** breakfast right now.

2 Jason, Stevie **isn't drinking** his milk.

3 Julia, you**'re not eating** your breakfast.

4 They**'re learning** a lot at school this year.

B Complete the sentences in the present continuous. Use an affirmative or negative form of the verbs in parentheses ( ).

1 He _____ (take) a bath. He's in the shower.

2 I _____ (do) my homework now. It's really difficult.

3 Carola isn't studying right now. She _____ (watch) TV.

4 My parents _____ (wash) the car. They're having lunch now.

5 I _____ (brush) my hair. I'm brushing my teeth.

6 You _____ (help) your friends with their English. You're really nice!

7 My cat loves milk. It _____ (drink) milk right now.

C ▶ Now go to page 135. Look at the grammar chart and do the grammar exercise for 7.1.

D Think about four of your friends. What are they doing or not doing now? Write sentences about each person. Then check your accuracy.

Teresa isn't studying. She's playing games on her phone.

✓ **ACCURACY** CHECK

Use the present continuous for things you're doing now. Use the simple present for things you do regularly.

Just a minute. ~~I talk~~ on the phone. ✗
Just a minute. I'm talking on the phone. ✓
I talk on the phone every day. ✓
I'm talking on the phone every day. ✗

---

4 SPEAKING

A Think of what you're usually doing at the times of day below. Is it a good or bad time to call you?

- Monday, 7:30 a.m.
- Tuesday, 10:00 a.m.
- Wednesday, 1:30 p.m
- Thursday, 3:30 p.m.
- Friday, 9:30 p.m
- Saturday, 11:00 a.m.
- Sunday, 6:00 p.m.

B PAIR WORK Take turns choosing times in exercise 4A. For each time, "call" your partner and ask, *"Is this a good time to call?"* Listen to the answers. Is your partner a busy person?

Hi, is this a good time to call?

No, sorry. I'm having dinner with my family.

TEXTING ON THE RUN

LESSON OBJECTIVE
■ ask and answer questions about travel

1 VOCABULARY: Transportation

A 🔊 2.04 **Look at the pictures. Listen and repeat.**

take the bus/
train/subway

go to a store / your
parents' house

walk

be at the bus stop /
train station

carry a bag

wait

ride your/my bike

be on the bus/train/subway

drive

B **Circle the correct words to complete the sentences.**

1 I *ride my bike / am at the bus stop* to class every day.

2 I'm *waiting / walking* for a friend right now.

3 We *are on the train / take the subway* to work on Fridays.

4 Are you *carrying / walking* right now?

5 I'm *at the train station / to the mall* right now.

C ▶ **Now do the vocabulary exercises for 7.2 on page 146.**

D GROUP WORK **How do you usually get to the places in the box? For ideas, watch Julieth's video.**

English class   the supermarket   work/college   your best friend's house

REAL STUDENT
Do you use the same transportation as Julieth?

2 LANGUAGE IN CONTEXT

A **Read the text messages. Where is Inna going? Why?**

B **Read the text messages again. Correct the sentences.**

1 Inna is sending text messages to ~~her father~~.   *Rob*

2 Inna is taking the bus to the mall.   _____

3 Inna's dad is waiting at his house.   _____

4 Inna is carrying a big bag.   _____

5 Today is Inna's dad's birthday.   _____

INSIDER ENGLISH

People often write *ha ha* (the sound of a laugh) in informal writing. It means they think something is funny.

12:00 PM

Hey, Inna. Are you going to work?

No, I'm not. **I'm on the bus**. I'm **going to my parents' house**.

You usually **ride your bike** there. Why are you **taking the bus**?

Because I'm **carrying** a big plant. Oh, **I'm at the bus stop** now, and my dad's **waiting**.

😄 Ha ha! A plant! Why are you carrying a plant?

Because plants don't **walk**! 😄😄😄 Really it's for my mom's birthday.

Oh, wow! Say happy birthday from me.

3 GRAMMAR: present continuous questions

A   (Circle) the correct answer. Use the questions in the grammar box to help you.

   1 Use *are* and *is* **at the beginning** / **in the middle** of *yes/no* questions.

   2 Use *are* and *is* **before** / **after** question words (for example, *What* or *When*) in information questions.

> ### Present continuous questions
>
> | *Yes/no* questions | Information questions |
> | --- | --- |
> | **Are** you **going** to work? | **Why is** he **carrying** a plant? |
> | **Is** she **carrying** a plant? | **Who are** they **waiting** for? |
> | **Are** they **waiting** at the bus stop? | **What are** you **doing**? |

B   Complete the questions with the present continuous form of the verbs in the box. Then match the questions and the answers below.

> carry   do   go   listen   ride

   1 _____ Josh _____ his bike in the park right now?

   2 What _____ Kim and Todd _____ ?

   3 _____ the children _____ to music right now?

   4 Why _____ Jamal _____ a big bag?

   5 Where _____ Lydia _____ now?

   ____ **a** Because he's taking a lot of books to class.

   ____ **b** Yes, they are.

   ____ **c** She's walking to her friend's house.

   ____ **d** No, he isn't. He's running by the lake.

   ____ **e** They're driving to the beach.

C   ▶ **Now go to page 135. Look at the grammar charts and do the grammar exercise for 7.2.**

D   PAIR WORK   **Imagine what people in your family are doing right now. Ask and answer questions.**

> What's your sister doing right now?

4 SPEAKING

FIND IT

A   **Imagine you're going somewhere and carrying something interesting or funny. Use the ideas below or your own ideas. Then decide where you are going and your transportation.**

> a big bag   a small chair   an expensive picture

B   PAIR WORK   **What is your partner doing? Ask and answer questions.**

> Hi, Anna. What are you doing?

> I'm carrying 100 cookies. I'm at the subway station.

1 FUNCTIONAL LANGUAGE

A **Look at the people. Are they having a long or a short conversation? How long are your phone calls?**

B 🔊 **2.05** **Luana is calling her friend Jennifer. Read and listen. What's new in Luana's life?**

🔊 **2.05 Audio script**

Jennifer	**Hello.**
Luana	**Hi**, Jennifer. **It's** Luana.
Jennifer	**Hey**, Luana!
Luana	**How's it going?**
Jennifer	**Not bad, thanks. How are you doing?**
Luana	**Good, thanks.** Well, I'm busy.
Jennifer	Really? What are you doing these days?
Luana	I have a new job, in Monterrey.
Jennifer	Oh, wow! *Monterrey*? So you're not living in Mexico City now.
Luana	That's right. I'm living in Monterrey. I live in a new building. It's expensive, but it's very nice. And I have a new boyfriend.
Jennifer	Really? Great! You have a new *life*! I want to hear all about it!

C **Complete the chart with expressions in bold from the conversation above.**

Answering the phone and greeting people	Asking people how they are	Responding
1 ___Hello___ .	How's it 5 _____ ?	
2 _____ , Jennifer.	(How's = How is)	Not 8 _____ , thanks.
3 _____ Luana.	How 6 _____ you	9 _____ , thanks.
4 _____ , Luana!	7 _____ ?	I'm fine.
	How are you?	

D 🔊 **2.06** PAIR WORK **Put the phone conversation in the correct order. Listen and check. Then practice with a partner.**

___ Good, thanks. How's it going?

_3_ Hey, Andrew! How are you doing?

_1_ Hello.

___ Not bad.

___ Hi, Francisco. It's Andrew.

2 REAL-WORLD STRATEGY

REACTING TO NEWS

People often say *oh* after they hear good news, ordinary news, and bad news.

Good news 😄

Oh, wow!

Ordinary news 😐

Oh.

Bad news 🙁

Oh, no!

Luana *I have a new job.*

Luana *I'm busy.*

Luana *My apartment is very expensive.*

Jennifer *Oh, wow!*

Jennifer *Oh.*

Jennifer *Oh, no!*

A Read the information in the box about reacting to news. Then look at the examples. What does Jennifer think is: good news, ordinary news, and bad news?

B 🔊 2.07 **Listen to a conversation. What news does the man give?**

Ordinary news: _____He's in his car._____ Good news: _____

Bad news: _____

C 🔊 2.07 **Listen again. How does the woman react to the different types of news?**

D ▶ PAIR WORK **Student A: Go to page 158. Student B: Go to page 160. Follow the instructions.**

3 PRONUNCIATION: Saying *-ing* at the end of the word

A 🔊 2.08 **Listen. Complete the words.**

1 How are you do_____?   2 I'm liv_____ in Dallas.   3 Where are you go_____?

B 🔊 2.09 **Listen. Focus on the *-in* and *-ing* sounds.** (Circle) **the phrase you hear.**

1 a learn in Spanish   b learning Spanish   4 a study in nature   b studying nature

2 a call in the restaurant b calling the restaurant   5 a carry in a bag   b carrying a bag

3 a help in my school   b helping my school   6 a shop in malls   b shopping malls

C 🔊 2.10 PAIR WORK **Listen to the conversations. Then practice with a partner. Listen for the *-ing* sound.**

1 **A** How are you do**ing**?

   B Not bad. I'm work**ing** in Monterrey now.

2 **A** Are you liv**ing** in Mexico City now?

   B No, I'm liv**ing** in Monterrey.

3 **A** Where are you go**ing**?

   B We're go**ing** to the Italian restaurant over there.

4 SPEAKING

PAIR WORK **Imagine you're calling your partner. Start the call, and then talk about some news. Use some of the questions below. React to the things your partner says. Then change roles.**

How are you doing?   Are you busy?

What are you doing right now?   What about you?

Hey, Ali. It's Clara.   Hey, Clara! How are you doing?

CHAOS!

1 READING

A **SKIM** Skim the text. Where is the man? What is on his laptop?

JAMIE'S BLOG

HOME   **ABOUT**   **BLOG**

Bloggers sometimes write from difficult places: mountains, deserts, rainforests …
So today, my blog is from a difficult place, too. I'm writing from my living room.

Why is it difficult to write in here? Well, my brother's playing soccer (yes, in the living room.) The ball is going *BOOM-BOOM-BOOM* on the wall near my table and chair. My sister's doing her homework. Every two minutes, she asks me a question: "What's 15% of 500? What's 50% of 320?" So, really, *I'm* doing her homework.

The TV is on, but I don't know why. My mom's talking about work on the phone, so she isn't watching TV. And my dad isn't watching it. He's in the kitchen: *PSSSSSS, CRASH, BANG!* He's cooking – I think. And the cat doesn't like TV. But she likes laptops. She's walking on my laptop … and now she's going to sleep! How do I work in this place? It's chaos!

B **READ FOR DETAILS** Read the blog again. Find words to complete the chart.

5 people in the family	*me*	
3 technology words		
2 pieces of furniture		
2 rooms		
1 animal		

C **PAIR WORK** **THINK CRITICALLY** Which people from exercise 1B are busy? having fun?

2 WRITING

A Jodi is a college student. She's helping at a school for a week. Read her blog. What <u>six</u> things are the children doing? What <u>three</u> things is Jodi doing? What <u>one</u> thing are the children <u>and</u> Jodi doing?

Jodi's Blog
Home   About   Blog

Busy!
April 11

I'm helping a teacher at a school this week. Today, I'm writing my blog on a school bus. We're going to the beach. There are 25 kids on the bus, and they're nine and ten years old. Wow, they're making a lot of noise! They're busy, too. Some kids are talking. Some kids are playing music on their phones. Some are singing. Three boys are playing games on a tablet. Also, the children are eating cookies.
What about me? Well, I'm cleaning their hands 🤚 and washing their faces 😊.
And I'm answering millions of questions from the kids. They're happy.
The teacher is happy, too.
But this is difficult for me.
Am I getting old? 😃

GLOSSARY
noise (*n*) a sound or sounds, usually loud
millions (*quantifier*) a lot (informal)

B WRITING SKILLS People use *also* and *too* to add information. <u>Underline</u> the words *also* and *too* in the blog. Then (circle) the correct words in the rules, below.
Use *too* at the **beginning** / **end** of a sentence.
Use a comma (,) **before** / **after** you write *too*.
Use *also* at the **beginning** / **end** *of a sentence.*
Use a *comma* (,) **before** / **after** you write *also*.

🕐 WRITE IT

C Imagine you're in a very busy place: at home, at college, at work, on a bus, or at a party. Write a blog about the activities happening around you. Use the title "Busy!"

D PAIR WORK Compare your blog with a partner. How many activities does your partner describe?

REGISTER CHECK

People sometimes use *And, Also,* or *But* at the beginning of sentences in speaking and informal writing. In formal writing, people usually don't begin sentences with these words.

And I'm answering millions of questions from the kids.

Also, the children are eating cookies.

But this is difficult for me.

7.5

TIME TO SPEAK
Your life these days

A **PREPARE** Read the note and questions below. Which topic is interesting for you? Which topic is boring?

You are with a group of people. They are your friends, but you hardly ever see them. What do you say? Here are some ideas!

Topics	Main question	Follow-up questions
Work and school	Are you going to college?	Are your classes easy or difficult? Are you doing a lot of homework these days?
	What classes are you taking?	Do you like your classes? Why or why not?
	Where are you working these days?	Are you working every day? Is your job interesting? Is it difficult?
Free time	What are you reading these days?	Is it good? Who's the writer?
	What are you watching on TV?	Is it interesting? Is it funny? Who's in it?
	What music are you listening to?	Who's your favorite singer? What's your favorite band?
	Do you play video games?	Which games are you playing right now?
	Are you going out a lot these days?	Where do you go? What's your favorite place?
	Are you playing sports?	What sports do you play? Where?
Home life	How is your family?	Are you living with them now?
	Are you living in a new place?	Is it an apartment or house? Do you like it? Is it close to work/school?
	Are you cooking a lot these days?	Do you cook for other people?

B **ROLE PLAY** Imagine you are at a party. Talk to different people about different topics. Ask and answer some of the questions from the chart.

C **AGREE** Talk about popular things from your conversations. What are a lot of people doing these days?

To check your progress, go to page 154.

USEFUL PHRASES

PREPARE
I like / don't like …
I think … is interesting/boring.
And you?

ROLE PLAY
Hi, [name]. How's it going?
Hey, [name]! What are you doing these days?

AGREE
(Work and school / free time / home life) is a popular topic.
A lot of people are doing …

74

UNIT OBJECTIVES
- talk about your skills and abilities
- say what you can and can't do at work or school
- say why you're the right person for a job
- write an online comment with your opinion
- talk about what people in your country are good at

YOU'RE GOOD!

8

START SPEAKING

A   Look at the picture. Where is this person? What is he doing?

B   Do you think this is a difficult activity? Do you think it's fun?

C   Talk to a partner about fun or difficult activities you do. For ideas, watch Anderson's video.

REAL STUDENT

What does Anderson do? Do you think it's fun, difficult, or both?

8.1 SHE LIKES MUSIC, BUT SHE CAN'T DANCE!

LESSON OBJECTIVE
- talk about your skills and abilities

1 VOCABULARY: Verbs to describe skills

A 🔊 **2.11 Listen and repeat the skills in the pictures. Which are fun skills? Which are difficult skills?**

 dance

 draw

 fix things

 read music

 paint

 play the guitar

 sing

 skateboard

 snowboard

 speak two languages

 surf

 swim

B ▶ **Now do the vocabulary exercises for 8.1 on page 147.**

2 LANGUAGE IN CONTEXT

A 🔊 **2.12 Read and listen. Who are Mia and her dad talking about? What do they choose to buy? Do you think it's a good idea?**

🔊 **2.12 Audio script**

Dad So, Mia. You know it's your mom's birthday next month, right?

Mia Oh wow! Let's buy her something really cool. Do you have any ideas?

Dad Hmm. How about some art classes? She can **draw**.

Mia Or what about singing lessons? She likes music and can **play the guitar**.

Dad I don't think that's a good idea. She thinks she can't **sing**, and she's very shy about it.

Mia Hmm. What about dance lessons? Can she **dance** well?

Dad No, she can't. She's terrible at it. It's really funny – she can **read music**, but she can't dance!

Mia *You* can't dance, Dad. I know! Let's buy you both some dance lessons!

Dad Great idea! Wait a minute – what?

INSIDER ENGLISH

You can use *So* to start talking about a topic.

So, Mia. You know it's your mom's birthday next month, right?

GLOSSARY
terrible (*adj*) very bad

B 🔊 **2.12 Read and listen again. What can Mia's mom do? What can't she do? Complete the sentences.**

1 Mia's mom can _____, _____, and _____ .

2 She can't _____ and _____ .

C **PAIR WORK** Talk to a partner. Which things in exercise 1A do you often do? Which things do you never do? For ideas, watch Larissa's video.

 REAL STUDENT

Do you often do the same things as Larissa?

3 GRAMMAR: *can* and *can't* for ability; *well*

A (Circle) the correct answers. Use the sentences in the grammar box and the information in the Notice box to help you.

1 Use *can / can't* to talk about things you don't do well or don't know how to do.

2 Use *can / can't* to talk about things you do well or know how to do.

3 With *he*, *she*, and *it*, **do / do not** add -s to the verb after *can* or *can't*.

can and *can't* (= *can not*) for ability

I **can** swim.	I **can't** play the guitar.	**Can** you fix things?
She **can** draw.	He **can't** sing well.	**Can** he surf?
We **can** surf well.	They **can't** read music.	**Can** they speak two languages?

> **!** *Well* is the adverb of *good*.
> *She can sing **well**.* (= she's good.)
> *I can't dance **well**.* (= I'm not good.)

B (Circle) the correct answers to complete the sentences.

1 I swim every day. I *can / can't* swim well.

2 Sorry. My dad *can / can't* fix your car. He's not a mechanic.

3 You can draw really well, Tomas. What other things *can / can't* you do?

4 She *can / can't* drive, and she doesn't have a car.

5 You *can / can't* skateboard really well! Can you teach me?

6 **A** Can you play the guitar, Robbie?

   B No, I *can / can't*.

C ▶ Now go to page 136. Look at the grammar chart and do the grammar exercise for 8.1.

D Write <u>five</u> questions to ask people in your class about their skills. Use vocabulary from exercise 1A. Then check your accuracy.

1 Can you _____ ?

2 Can you _____ ?

3 Can you _____ ?

4 Can you _____ ?

5 Can you _____ ?

> ✓ **ACCURACY** CHECK
>
> Do <u>not</u> use *to* between *can/can't* and a verb.
> Can you ~~to~~ fix bikes? ✗
> Can you fix bikes? ✓

4 SPEAKING

A [GROUP WORK] **Ask and answer your questions from exercise 3D. Say how well you do the skills.**

Can you play the guitar?

No, I can't. What about you?

Yes, I can. I can play it really well.

B [GROUP WORK] **What skill can everyone in your group do? Who can do it really well?**

77

8.2 HAPPY WORKERS = GREAT WORKERS?

LESSON OBJECTIVE
- say what you can and can't do at work or school

1 LANGUAGE IN CONTEXT

A Look at the offices in the pictures on pages 78 and 79. How are they different from other offices? Do you like them? Are they good places to work?

B Read the article. What activities can you do in a happy office?

Not just an office ... an ☺FFICE

Who can you find in all great **companies**? Great **workers**. And what's true for all great workers? They're happy because happy people do a great job.

How can companies make their workers happy? They can pay them a lot of money, of course, but money can't make people happy – not always. A great company can also give its workers a happy **office**. Happy offices aren't just ordinary offices with desks, phones, and computers – and they're not *just* for work.

What can you do in a happy office? The short answer is, you can **work hard** *and* have fun. You can run or play basketball with **your coworkers** and **have a meeting** at the same time. This is a great way to **think** of new ideas. You can work in a cool room with big chairs and no table or **take a break** in a room with a lot of plants (like a forest!) In some offices, you can come to work with your dog!

GLOSSARY
all (*det*) 100% of something
pay (*v*) give someone money for their work
ordinary (*adj*) usual, normal

2 VOCABULARY: Work

A 🔊 2.13 Find the words below in the article. Then listen and repeat.

| company | workers | office | work hard | have a meeting | think | take a break | your coworkers |

B Match the words from exercise 2A with the definitions.

1 a workplace, with desks and chairs

2 the people you work with

3 a business – for example, Microsoft or Toyota

4 the people in a company

5 do a lot of work

6 stop work for a short time – for example, to have coffee

7 have ideas, or find answers to problems

8 get together with people at work and talk about business

C ▶ Now do the vocabulary exercises for 8.2 on page 148.

FIND IT

D GROUP WORK What other activities can you do in a happy office? Which companies have happy workers? You can go online to find examples.

3 GRAMMAR: *can* and *can't* for possibility

A   Circle the correct answers. Use the sentences in the grammar box to help you.

1   Use *can* to talk about things that are **possible** / **not possible**.

2   Question words (*Who, What, Where, Why,* and *How*) go **before** / **after** *can* or *can't* to ask about possibility.

> ### *can* and *can't* for possibility
>
> You **can** work hard and have fun.
> She **can** take a break any time.
> Your dog **can't** come to work with you.
>
> What **can't** they do in the office?
> How **can** companies make their workers happy?
> Where **can** you have a meeting?

B   Put the words in the correct order to make questions. Then match them to the answers (a–e) below.

1   we / have / lunch? / can / Where _____

2   the / restaurant? / How / get / to / can / I _____

3   can / What / eat? / we _____

4   have / the / meeting? / we / can / When _____

5   I / this / message? / send / can / How _____

____   **a**   We can have some cookies.

____   **b**   You can email it from your phone.

____   **c**   Tuesday is good for me.

____   **d**   In the company restaurant.

____   **e**   Go straight, and then turn left.

C   ▶ Now go to page 137. Look at the grammar chart and do the grammar exercise for 8.2.

D   Write questions about a company or school to ask if it's a good place to work or study.

1   What can _____ ?

2   Where can _____ ?

3   How can _____ ?

4 SPEAKING

PAIR WORK   **Talk to a partner about things you can and can't do at your company or school. Ask your questions from exercise 3D.**

> What can you do at lunchtime?

> You can go to …

8.3 ARE YOU THE RIGHT PERSON?

1 FUNCTIONAL LANGUAGE

A **Look at the picture. Where are the people? What are they doing?**

B 🔊 **2.14 Read and listen. What three things can the man do well?**

> 🔊 **2.14 Audio script**
>
> A   Can we speak in English for five minutes?
>
> B   Yes, we can.
>
> A   Great. So, are you the right person for this job?
>
> B   Yes. **I think so.**
>
> A   Why? In a very short answer, please.
>
> B   Because I can work well with people on a team. **I think that** teamwork is very important.
>
> A   I see. **Why do you think** it's important?
>
> B   Because a company is a big team. I mean, it's a group of people, and you work with them every day.
>
> A   And why are *you* good on a team?
>
> B   Because I like people, and I can communicate well.
>
> A   That's great. **I think that** good communication is important. But **I don't think** it's the only important thing. What other things can you do well?
>
> B   I can speak two languages. I mean, I speak Spanish and English.

C **Complete the chart with expressions in bold from the conversation above.**

Asking for opinions	Giving opinions
What do you think ? ¹ _____ do you think (that) … ?	I think ² _____ . I don't think so. I ³ _____ (that) … I ⁴ _____ think (that) …

D 🔊 **2.15** **PAIR WORK** **Complete the conversations with words from exercise 1C. Listen and check. Then ask and answer the questions with a partner. Answer with your ideas.**

1 A I think video games are great. What do you think?

   B I _____ they're very cool. They're boring.

2 A _____ do you _____ cell phones are important?

   B They're useful. We communicate with our phones.

3 A Do you think soccer is a good sport?

   B No. I _____ . I like basketball.

4 A Are you good at music?

   B I _____ . I sing and play the guitar really well.

2 REAL-WORLD STRATEGY

EXPLAINING AND SAYING MORE ABOUT AN IDEA

Use *I mean* to explain or say more about an idea.

A company is a big team. I mean, it's a group of people, and you work with them every day.

I can speak two languages. I mean, I speak Spanish and English.

A Read about explaining and saying more about an idea in the box above. Look at what the man says. What idea does he explain? What idea does he give more information about?

B 🔊 **2.16** Listen to a conversation. What does Lori want to do? When does she have free time?

C 🔊 **2.16** Listen to the conversation again. Complete the chart with the sentences you hear.

Idea	Explanation/more information
I work really hard.	I mean, I ¹_____ about ²_____ a day.
I'm not busy.	I mean, I ³_____ in a restaurant ⁴_____ _____ , but I have free time in the ⁵_____ .

D ▶ | PAIR WORK | **Student A: Go to page 158. Student B: Go to page 160. Follow the instructions.**

3 PRONUNCIATION: Saying groups of words

A 🔊 **2.17** **Listen for the space (= short pause) between the words (/). Which sentences do you hear, A or B?**

1 **A** Can we speak in English / for five minutes?

   B Can we speak in / English for five minutes?

2 **A** What other things can / you do well?

   B What other things / can you do well?

B 🔊 **2.18** **Listen to the sentences. Write a pause mark (/) in each sentence.**

1 I'm good on a team because I can communicate well.

2 I can speak two languages and I can play the guitar.

3 I work in a restaurant at night but I'm free in the mornings.

4 I think that good communication is important but I don't think it's the only important thing.

C | PAIR WORK | **Practice the sentences in exercise 3B with a partner. Take turns. Can your partner hear the spaces between the words?**

4 SPEAKING

A **Choose a job from the box or your own idea. Think about why you are the right person for the job.**

> an art teacher   a chef at a restaurant   a hotel clerk
> a singer in a band   a soccer player

B | PAIR WORK | **Tell a partner your job from exercise 4A. Your partner interviews you for the job. Then change roles.**

> Are you the right person for this job?   I think so. I …

8.4 COMPUTERS AND OUR JOBS

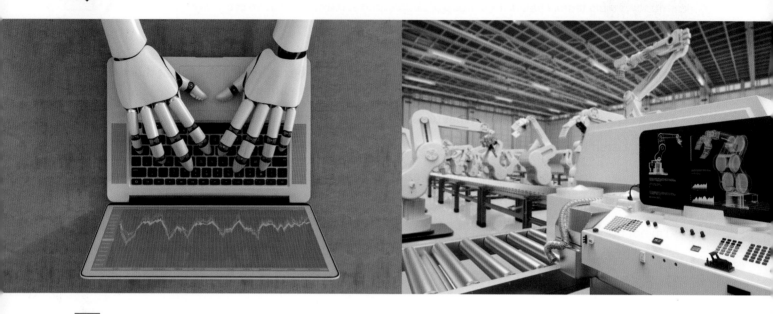

1 LISTENING

A Chris is the host of the podcast *Technology Talks*. Look at the pictures above. What is today's podcast about?

B ◀ㅇ 2.19 LISTEN FOR DETAILS Listen to the podcast. Who is Joanna Ramos? What does she say computers <u>can't</u> do?

C ◀ㅇ 2.19 LISTEN FOR SUPPORTING DETAILS Listen again. Check (✓) the supporting details Joanna gives.

Jobs for computers	New jobs for people
☐ make cars	☐ make computers
☐ drive cars	☐ start computer companies
☐ call people on the phone	☐ make cars
☐ talk	☐ be a computer's voice
☐ think	☐ make phones

D PAIR WORK THINK CRITICALLY Who thinks computers are a good thing: Joanna or Chris?

2 PRONUNCIATION: Listening for *can* and *can't*

A ◀ㅇ 2.20 Listen. Write the missing words.

1 What _____ computers do?

2 They _____ make cars.

3 A computer _____ make 100% of a car.

B ◀ㅇ 2.21 Listen. Do you hear *can* or *can't*? Circle the correct words.

1 can / can't   2 can / can't

3 can / can't   4 can / can't

WRITING

A   Read three people's online comments about the podcast. Which person thinks Joanna is correct? Which person <u>doesn't</u> think Joanna is correct? What's your favorite comment?

TECHNOLOGY TALKS:
Interview with Joanna Ramos

JUNE 1, 11:30 A.M.

Kaito, Tokyo

I don't think Joanna Ramos is right. Computers *are* a problem. Robots are taking all our jobs! They can say hello to people in stores and hotels, they can cook, they can play music, they can clean buildings, they can make cars … What jobs CAN'T they do? Joanna says, "People make computers." Well, I think robots can make computers now. They're *very* smart.

Ruby, Miami

Computers and robots can do a lot of things, but they don't have feelings: they're not happy, and they're not sad. Feelings are important for many jobs. For example, teachers, doctors, and nurses work with people, so feelings are important. I don't like the idea of robot doctors!

Arturo, Mexico City

Computers are cheap. I mean, companies pay people for their work, but they don't pay their robots or computers. And computers work hard. But I think Ruby is right. Computers don't have feelings. Joanna is right, too. She says, "They are taking *some* of our jobs." Not *all* of them. She also says, "There are a lot of new jobs, too." That's true. It's not a problem.

GLOSSARY

robot (*n*) a machine with a computer in it

B   **WRITING SKILLS** Sometimes we want to write another person's words. Their words are quotations. Read the rules below. Then (circle) all the capital letters and punctuation marks in sentences 1–3.

- Use quotation marks (" ") around other people's words.
- Put a comma (,) after *says*.
- Start the quotation with a capital letter (A, B, C, …).

1   Joanna says, "People make computers."
2   She says, "They are taking *some* of our jobs."
3   She also says, "There are a lot of new jobs, too."

REGISTER CHECK

In informal writing and speaking, people often use *says* to quote (= give) another person's words.

In an online comment: *Joanna says, "People make computers."*

In formal writing, people often use *said*.

In a newspaper article: *Joanna Ramos said, "A computer can't make 100% of a car."*

 WRITE IT

C   Read the ideas from Joanna's interview in exercise 1C. Then write an online comment. Give your opinion about computers and jobs. Quote some of Joanna's words.

D   GROUP WORK   Read your group's comments. Do you have the same or different ideas?

8.5

TIME TO SPEAK
National skills

A **PREPARE** Match the skills in the box to the pictures. Which three skills are <u>not</u> in the pictures?

| cook | dance | make movies | paint | play soccer | sing | snowboard | surf |

B **DISCUSS** Where can people do the things from exercise A really well? For each skill, say the name of a city, region/area, or country. Then compare your ideas with your group.

C **DECIDE** Read the information in the box on the right. Talk to a partner about the question in the box. Together, think of <u>three</u> skills for the video.

D **AGREE** Compare everyone's ideas. Choose your class' <u>three</u> favorite ideas for the video.

 To check your progress, go to page 154.

CAN YOU HELP US?
We want to make a YouTube™ video about our country and why it's great. The title is "We're good!" The video is about the skills people have here. What can we do *really* well in this country? Please send us your ideas!

USEFUL PHRASES

 DISCUSS
Where can people cook really well?
Chinese food is always great.
I think people can cook really well in Rome and Naples.
What do you think?

 DECIDE
What can we do really well in this country?
We can do … well.
I agree. / I disagree.
Our three skills for the video are …

 AGREE
What are your ideas?
Good idea!
Our three favorite skills are …

UNIT OBJECTIVES
- talk about travel and vacations
- make travel plans
- ask for information in a store
- write a description of a place
- plan a vacation for someone

PLACES TO GO

9

START SPEAKING

A   Look at the picture. Where is the woman? Is it difficult to get to this place?

B   What do you do in your free time? Do you go to new places?

C   Think of a place you like. Talk about it. Say why it's good. For ideas, watch Julieth's video.

REAL STUDENT

What's Julieth's place? Do you agree it's a good place to go?

9.1 I LOVE IT HERE!

1 LANGUAGE IN CONTEXT

A **Kaitlin and her friends are on vacation. Read Kaitlin's posts. Where do they go?**

B **Read again. Check (✓) the sentences that are true. Correct the false ones.**

☐ 1 Kaitlin takes a bus to San Diego.

☐ 2 They go to their hotel on Thursday.

☐ 3 They are in San Diego on Friday.

☐ 4 They go to a zoo on Saturday.

☐ 5 Kaitlin and her friends have a bad vacation.

● ● ● ⟨ ⟩   🔍 🏠

FROM MY SMALL **TOWN** TO A BIG **CITY**

👤 PROFILE
▶ LOG OUT

THURSDAY MORNING

Goodbye to my small **town**. San Diego, here I come! I have my **ticket** and my seat on the **plane**. I'm next to the window!

THURSDAY AFTERNOON

Now I'm in San Diego, and this is our hotel. These are my friends in front of the hotel.

FRIDAY

Today we're in the **country**, not in the **city**! We're at this cool **ranch** near San Diego. It's a really big **farm**.

SATURDAY

We're at the San Diego Zoo. These birds are funny. They're talking. They say, "Hello. How are you? Hello. How are you?" 🦜🦜🦜

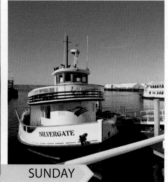

SUNDAY

Now I'm on a **tour** of San Diego Bay. I'm on a **boat** with my friends. They're not listening to the tour guide because they're talking.

A fun **vacation**? I think so. I love it here! 😄

GLOSSARY

tour guide (*n*) this person takes you to a place and tells you about it

2 VOCABULARY: Travel

A 🔊 **2.22** **Listen and repeat the words. Which words are places?**

| boat | country | farm | plane | ranch | ticket | tour | town | vacation |

B ▶ **Now do the vocabulary exercises for 9.1 on page 148.**

C PAIR WORK **Which places do you like from Kaitlin's vacation? Which places <u>don't</u> you like? Why?**

3 GRAMMAR: *This* and *These*

A (Circle) the correct answer. Use the sentences in the grammar box to help you.

1 Use *This bird* and *These birds* to talk about **birds around you / birds you can't see**.

2 *This* and *these* go **before / after** a noun.

3 ***This / these*** goes before a singular noun. ***This / these*** goes before a plural noun.

4 You **can / can't** use *this* and *these* at the beginning of a sentence.

This and These

This ticket is expensive.   **These** birds are funny.

We're at **this** cool ranch.   I don't like **these** pictures.

B Kaitlin writes a postcard about a museum. Write *this* or *these* to complete Kaitlin's postcard.

Dear Grandma,

I'm in San Diego! It's great. ¹ _____ postcard shows Balboa Park in the city. The park is very big, and it has 15 museums! ² _____ museums are for art, technology, transportation, and history. We're at the Mingei International Museum right now. You can see it in ³ _____ photo on the right. ⁴ _____ museum is interesting because it has local art – the artists are from ⁵ _____ city. I'm looking at some cool pictures now. ⁶ _____ pictures show places in San Diego. ⁷ _____ artists are *really* good. ⁸ _____ is my favorite room in the museum.

Love, Kaitlin

San Diego

C ▶ Now go to page 137. Look at the grammar chart and do the grammar exercise for 9.1.

4 SPEAKING

FIND IT

A Choose five pictures on your phone or draw some simple pictures of places you know. Think about the people and places in the pictures.

B PAIR WORK Tell your partner about your pictures.

> This is a picture of my mom and my aunt. They're walking in the country. This hill is very big. What else? This is my favorite aunt. She's…

9.2 SAN FRANCISCO, HERE WE COME

LESSON OBJECTIVE
■ make travel plans

1 LANGUAGE IN CONTEXT

A ◀)) **2.23** Kaitlin is making a vacation video. Read and listen. Where is she now? Where is she going? How is she going there?

B ◀)) **2.23** Read and listen again. Check (✓) the sentences that are true. Correct the false ones.

☐ **1** The plane is expensive, and the bus is cheap.

☐ **2** You can take a bus to San Francisco at night.

☐ **3** It's Friday night. Kaitlin is sleeping in a hotel.

2 VOCABULARY: Travel arrangements

A ◀)) **2.24** Listen and repeat the sentences. Then match the sentences (a–h) to the pictures (1–8.)

a Stay in a hotel. ___

b Arrive at the airport. ___

c Check in at the airport. ___

d Fly to another airport. You can sleep on the flight. ___

e Leave your house. Ready to travel? ___

f Have a great trip! ___

g Arrive at your destination. ___

h Buy tickets online. ___

Hello again from San Diego! Today is Tuesday, and we want to **leave** on Friday. Our **destination** is San Francisco. But how do we **travel**? Do we **fly** or take the bus?

Well, the **flight** is two hours. But you have to **arrive** at the **airport** a long time before the flight. You need to **check in** two hours before. So in total, by plane, the **trip** is about five hours. That's not bad. And I like to fly. *But …* the ticket is expensive.

The bus *isn't* expensive. It *is* a long trip – it's 12 hours. But we can take a night bus. And it arrives in San Francisco the next morning. That's good because we don't need to **stay** in a hotel on Friday night.

So, we're taking the bus. We just need to buy our tickets **online**. And then, San Francisco, here we come … on the bus.

B ▶ Now do the vocabulary exercises for 9.2 on page 149.

C PAIR WORK Imagine you're going from San Diego to San Francisco. What's a good way to go? Why?

3 GRAMMAR: *like to, want to, need to, have to*

A (Circle) the correct answer. Use the sentences in the grammar box to help you.

1 Use *want to* + verb and *like to* + verb to talk about **necessary things / things you choose to do**.

2 Use *need to* + verb and *have to* + verb to talk about **necessary things / things you choose to do**.

3 After *like to*, *want to*, *need to*, and *have to*, use **verb + -ing / verb**.

> ### *like to, want to, need to, have to*
>
> I **like to** fly.
>
> You **need to** check in before the flight.
>
> We **want to** leave on Friday.
>
> She **wants to** take a bus.
>
> He **has to** buy tickets.
>
> My mom **likes to** sleep on a flight.

B (Circle) the correct answer to complete the sentences.

1 I always sit by the window because I *need to / like to* look outside. It's interesting!

2 My cell phone isn't old, but I *need to / want to* buy a new one.

3 My wife isn't happy because she *has to / wants to* work this weekend.

4 On Fridays, we *like to / need to* watch TV after dinner.

5 He starts work at 6:30, so he *needs to / wants to* get up really early.

C ▶ Now go to page 138. Look at the grammar chart and do the grammar exercise for 9.2.

D PAIR WORK Write <u>four</u> sentences that are true for you. Use *like to*, *want to*, *need to*, and *have to*. Then compare your sentences with a partner and check your accuracy.

> ✓ **ACCURACY** CHECK
>
> Use *to* with *want, like, need* and *have* when they are before another verb.
>
> I like fly. ✗
> I like to fly. ✓

4 SPEAKING

A Work alone. Imagine you have to take a trip for one of these reasons: vacation, work, or to visit family. Where do you want to go? How do you want to travel: on a bus, a train, or a plane? For ideas, watch Larissa's video.

REAL STUDENT *Do you want to travel the same way as Larissa?*

B PAIR WORK Tell your partner about your trip. Talk about the things you need to do for your trip.

I have to take a trip for work.

Where do you have to go?

Buenos Aires, and I want to go by plane. I like to fly.

You can buy your ticket online …

9.3 THEY'RE TWO FOR $15

1 FUNCTIONAL LANGUAGE

A 🔊 2.25 Andy arrives at the airport in Mexico City. Read and listen. What does he want to buy? What does he want to drink? What place does he ask about?

🔊 2.25 Audio script

Andy	Hello. I need a travel guide for Mexico City. **Where are the travel guides?**
Clerk	Sorry, can you say that again?
Andy	Travel guides – where are the travel guides?
Clerk	Oh, OK. They're here, with the books and magazines.
Andy	OK. **How much is that?**
Clerk	It's $9.99.
Andy	Great. I need to buy a travel guide for Guadalajara, too. **Is it the same price, $9.99?**
Clerk	Yes, it is. But good news! **They're two for $15.**
Andy	Great! I want both, please. Hey, **what time does the café open?** I really need some coffee.
Clerk	**It opens in about 10 minutes.**
Andy	OK. **And where is the men's restroom?**
Clerk	It's over there, next to the café. But first you need to buy your books!

INSIDER ENGLISH

People often say *restroom* in public places and *bathroom* in people's homes. *Restroom* is more polite.

At an airport:
Where is the men's restroom?

At a friend's house:
Sorry, where's your bathroom?

GLOSSARY

travel guide (*n*) a book with information about where to go and what to see in a city or country

B Complete the chart with expressions in **bold** from the conversation above.

Asking for information	Giving information
1 _____ the travel guides?	6 _____ $9.99.
2 _____ that?	7 _____ $15.
3 _____ , $9.99?	8 _____ about 10 minutes.
4 _____ the café open?	
5 _____ the men's restroom?	

C 🔊 2.26 Complete the conversations with words from the chart above. Listen and check.

1 **A** Excuse me. _____ is this smartwatch?

   B _____ $125.49.

   A What about this big smartwatch? Is it the _____ ?

   B No, it isn't. _____ $149.00.

2 **A** _____ flight 248 arrive?

   B It arrives _____ 30 minutes.

   A OK, thanks. Oh, and _____ the women's _____ ?

   B It's over there.

2 REAL-WORLD STRATEGY

ASKING SOMEONE TO REPEAT SOMETHING

To hear information again, ask, *Sorry, can you say that again?* or *Can you repeat that, please?*

Andy   *Where are the travel guides?*

Clerk   *Sorry, can you say that again?*

A   Read the information in the box. What question does the clerk ask? Why?

B   🔊 **2.27** Listen to a conversation. Does the woman understand the man the first time? What question does she ask? How much is the cell phone?

3 PRONUNCIATION: Saying prices

A   🔊 **2.28** Listen and repeat the prices. Where does the speaker put stress in each price?

1	$6.19 / $6.90	**3**	$17.30 / $70.13	**5**	$2.16 / $2.60
2	$15 / $50	**4**	$19 / $90	**6**	$14 / $40

B   🔊 **2.29** Listen and write the prices. Then practice the conversation with a partner.

A I love that picture! How much is it?

B It's $_____ .

A $_____ ! That's cheap!

B No, it's $_____ .

A Oh …

C   PAIR WORK   Work with a partner. Ask to buy your friend's cell phone, bag, or Student's Book. Make a mistake with the price. Use the conversation in exercise 3B for an example. Then change roles.

4 SPEAKING

FIND IT

PAIR WORK   Imagine you want to buy something. Look at the items below, or go online and find an item. Take turns being the customer. Ask for information, and ask the store clerk to repeat something. Then change roles.

$29.99, or two for $50

$6, or two for $10.50

$13, or two for $20

$45, or two for $79

Excuse me. How much is this mug?

It's $6, or two for $10.50.

Sorry, can you repeat that, please?

A GREAT DESTINATION

1 READING

A **RECOGNIZE TEXT TYPE** **Read the text. What is it from?**

☐ a travel guide   ☐ an email   ☐ a review   ☐ a student's homework

✈ TravelSmart PLACES TO GO **NEAR PUNO**

TAQUILE ISLAND

Taquile Island is in Lake Titicaca in Peru. You can see mountains in Bolivia from the island. About 2,000 people live on this interesting island.

TRANSPORTATION

You have to take a boat to the island from Puno. You can go with a tour company, or you can get a local boat. You are on the boat for about three hours. There are no cars on the island, so you have to walk after you arrive. It's a 40-minute walk to the town, and you can see a lot of nature on the way.

WHERE TO STAY

There are a small number of hotels on Taquile Island. You need to reserve a room before your trip. Prices are from $20 to $60 a night. You can also stay with a local family for about $9.

THINGS TO DO

- You can see dances in the town.
- You can eat at a restaurant or have lunch with a local family.
- The market has a lot of things to see, buy, and eat.

18

GLOSSARY

local (*adj*) from the nearby area or neighborhood
reserve (a room) (*v*) book or pay for a room before you travel to a place

B **SCAN** **Find the numbers in the text. What do these numbers mean?**

2,000   three   40 $20 to $60 $9

C **READ FOR DETAILS** **Read the text again. Circle the correct answers.**

1 Taquile Island *is / isn't* in Bolivia.

2 You *can / can't* get a boat to the island.

3 You *can / can't* drive on the island.

4 There are *no / some* hotels on the island.

5 There *are / aren't* restaurants on the island.

6 You *can / can't* meet local people.

D **PAIR WORK** **THINK CRITICALLY** **Why do people like to go to Taquile Island? Do you want to go there? Why or why not? Give examples from the text to explain your answer.**

2 WRITING

A Read Cameron's review of Taquile Island. What does he say <u>not</u> to do?

Taquile Island
Lake Titicaca, Puno, Peru

DestinationsNow   About | Hotels | Restaurants   Search

Reviews (365)   Write a review

Very good	673
Good	575
OK	6
Bad	0
Very bad	0

Search review topics

Cameron T.   ★★★★★ 3 weeks ago

You have to see Taquile Island!

This island is really nice. It's not very big. There is only one town on the island. There are a lot of small homes on the hills, and there's a lot of nature. I like to walk, and you have to walk a lot on Taquile. Walk to the top of the island and see the ocean. You can see Peru on one side and Bolivia on the other side. You can even see snow on the mountains in Bolivia. Don't take a tour with a travel company. Take a local boat and stay with a family. The people are very friendly. You don't need to eat at the restaurants in town. The food is OK, but the family gives you a great breakfast, lunch, and dinner. Talk with the family. You can learn a lot about Taquile this way. Don't forget your camera. You can take a lot of pictures of this wonderful place!

GLOSSARY
wonderful (*adj*) really good

B WRITING SKILLS Read the information about imperative verbs below. Then <u>underline</u> all the sentences beginning with an imperative verb in Cameron's review in exercise 2A.

You can use imperative verbs to give someone advice. An imperative verb is a verb with no subject (e.g. *he*, *she*).

+ **Walk** to the top of the island and see the ocean.

– **Don't take** a tour with a travel company.

WRITE IT

REGISTER CHECK

People often use imperative verbs in informal writing to give advice.

In a website review: *Walk to the top of the island.*

People usually use verb forms with subjects in formal writing.

In a travel guide: *You can walk to the top of the island.*

C Choose a place for people to visit in your area. Write a review of the place. Say what people can do and see. Use imperative verbs to give advice. Use Cameron's review in exercise 2A for an example.

D PAIR WORK Read your partner's review. Do you want to visit your partner's place? Why or why not?

9.5 TIME TO SPEAK
Vacation plans

A **DISCUSS** Look at the pictures. What do you think these people like to do on vacation? For each person, say <u>three</u> things. Compare your ideas with a partner. Find a new idea for each person.

Jim

Minako

Carter

B **DECIDE** Work in pairs. Choose Jim, Minako, or Carter. Imagine they are coming to your country on vacation for two weeks. What do you think they want to do? Make a list of things to do and places to go.

C **PREPARE** Imagine you are helping this person plan a vacation. Look at your list from exercise B. What do you need to do? Make a plan.

D **AGREE** Work in groups: Group Jim, Group Minako, or Group Carter. Present your plan. Which plan is your group's favorite?

 To check your progress, go to page 154.

USEFUL PHRASES

 DISCUSS
I think Jim/Minako/Carter likes to … on vacation.
What do you think Jim/Minako/Carter likes to do?
My three ideas for Jim are …
I agree. / I disagree.
Let's think of one new idea for Minako.

 DECIDE
A good thing to do / place to go is …
On the first day, he/she can …

 AGREE
We're planning a vacation for …
This is our plan.
Our favorite plan is … because it's interesting/fun/nice.

REVIEW 3 (UNITS 7–9)

1 VOCABULARY

A Write the words in the chart. There are <u>five</u> words or phrases for each group.

airport	clean my room	do homework	paint	take a break
be on the subway	company	draw	play the guitar	take the bus
brush my hair	dance	have a meeting	sing	do the dishes
check in	destination	office	take a bath	workers

Activities around the house	Transportation/Travel	Skills	Work

B Add <u>one</u> more word or phrase to each group in exercise 1A.

2 GRAMMAR

A Put the words in the correct order to make sentences.

1 my / right / cleaning / I'm / room / now. _____

2 aren't / homework. / The / doing / children / their _____

3 bus? / Is / waiting / she / a / for _____

4 days. / hard / is / these / father / My / working _____

5 watching / TV / not / right now. / They're _____

6 you / these / reading / What / days? / books / are _____

B PAIR WORK Tell a partner two or three things you are doing these days. For example, what you're reading or watching on TV, what classes you're taking, or what games/sports you're playing.

C Complete the sentences with *can* or *can't*.

1 My brother usually goes out for dinner because he _____ cook.

2 I _____ swim really well. I usually swim in the evening after work.

3 Juan _____ speak four languages: Spanish, Portuguese, French, and Italian.

4 My sister _____ skateboard, and she doesn't want to learn.

5 I _____ drive a car. It's easy.

6 My grandfather _____ use a computer. He doesn't have one, and he doesn't want one.

D PAIR WORK Talk to a partner. Say <u>two</u> things you can do and <u>two</u> things you can't do.

3 SPEAKING

A [PAIR WORK] **You're going to play a guessing game with your partner. Follow the instructions.**

1 Work alone. Choose one of these places, but <u>don't</u> tell your partner: in a room at home, in an office, in a classroom, on a train or a bus, in a car. Now, imagine you're in the place.

2 Talk to your partner. Say what you can and can't do in the place. Say what you're doing there now.

3 Your partner guesses the place. You can say *"Yes."* or *"No."*

> I can sleep here, and I can use my phone. I can't cook here, but I can go places. Right now, I'm studying here.

> Is it a classroom?

> No!

B **Write about your partner's place in exercise 3A. Describe what he/she can and can't do there.**

4 FUNCTIONAL LANGUAGE

A (Circle) **the correct answers.**

Robert   Hi, Marina! [1] *I'm / It's* Robert.

Marina   Hey, Robert! How are you [2] *do / doing*?

Robert   Not [3] *bad / fine*, thanks. And you?

Marina   [4] *I'm / It's* fine. What are you doing these days?

Robert   Well, I'm planning a trip to Rio for five days.

Marina   [5] *Oh, wow! / Oh no!* That's great!

Robert   Yeah, and the hotel's a good price.

Marina   Really? [6] *How much / When* is it?

Robert $189.99 a night.

Marina   [7] *I don't think / I think* that's a good price. That's really, really expensive!

Robert   [8] *I think / I think so* it's good. [9] *I mean / I say*, it's a five-star hotel.

Marina   [10] *Oh. / Oh no!* [11] *Where / What* is it?

Robert   In Copacabana.

5 SPEAKING

A [PAIR WORK] **Choose <u>one</u> of the situations below. Talk to a partner. Have a conversation.**

1 Start a telephone conversation. Ask how your partner is and what he/she is doing these days. Look at page 70 for useful language.

> Hi, Ji-un. How are you?

2 Talk about things people do in unusual offices. Give your opinion about these things. Look at page 80 for useful language.

> In some offices, you can play computer games. I don't think that's a good idea. I mean, people need to work!

3 You're at an airport and need information about prices, locations, and times. Look at page 90 for useful language.

> Excuse me. How much are these travel guides?

B [PAIR WORK] **Change roles and repeat the situation.**

UNIT OBJECTIVES

- make outdoor plans for the weekend
- discuss what clothes to wear for different trips
- suggest plans for evening activities
- write an online invitation
- plan and present a fun weekend in your city

GET READY

10

START SPEAKING

A   Look at the picture. Imagine you're doing this.
Say things you can do to get ready before you do it.

B   Do you have big plans for the future? What are they?
For ideas, watch Larissa's video.

REAL STUDENT

Are your plans the same as Larissa's?

WHITE NIGHTS

Midnight in St. Petersburg

To: sofiaperez@mymail.com
From: averin.yana@grabmail.org
Subject: Your trip

Reply   Forward

Hi Sofia,

You're going to be here next weekend! I'm very happy because you're going to see St. Petersburg during the White Nights. It's light for about 24 hours in June. We live *outside* – all day and *all night*.

So, here's the plan. On Friday evening, I'm going to **meet** you at the airport and then **take** you out to dinner. We're going to **eat** outside at Marketplace. It's my favorite restaurant.

On Saturday, we're going to **look at** art at the Street Art Museum. And, of course, we can **go** shopping on Nevsky Prospect. And then in the evening, we're going to **get together** with some of my friends in Kirov Park. We can **take** a walk in the park, and then we're going to **have** a picnic – at midnight!

What else do you want to do? I'm not going to be home tonight, but we can talk tomorrow.

See you soon!

Yana

GLOSSARY
light (*adj*) the sun is in the sky

---

1   LANGUAGE IN CONTEXT

A   PAIR WORK   **Look at the picture. Where is it? What time is it? What's unusual about it?**

B   **Read the email and answer the questions.**

1   Why is Yana happy?

2   What are the "White Nights"?

3   When does Yana want to talk to Sofia?

2   VOCABULARY: Going out

A   🔊 2.30   **Find these verbs in the email. Then complete the phrases with the verbs. Listen and check.**

| eat   get together   go   have   look at   meet   take (2x) |

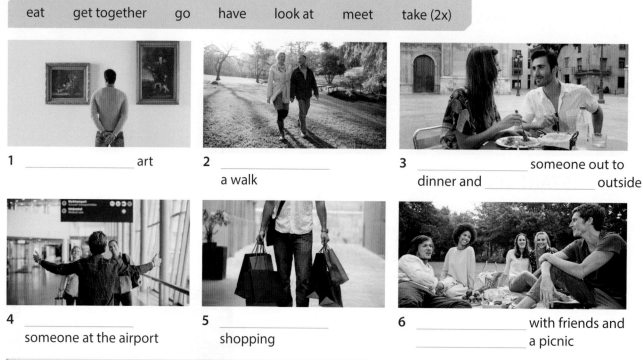

1 _____ art

2 _____ a walk

3 _____ someone out to dinner and _____ outside

4 _____ someone at the airport

5 _____ shopping

6 _____ with friends and _____ a picnic

B   ▶ **Now do the vocabulary exercises for 10.1 on page 149.**

C   GROUP WORK   **How often do you do the activities in exercise 2A? Tell your group.**

3 GRAMMAR: Statements with *be going to*

A **Circle the correct answer. Use the sentences in the grammar box to help you.**

1 Use *be going to* to talk about **things you're doing right now / future plans**.

2 Make future statements with *be going to* + **a verb / a noun**.

> **Statements with *be going to***
>
> I'**m going to be** home tomorrow.　　　　　　I'**m not going to be** home tonight.
>
> It'**s going to be** light all night.　　　　　　It **isn't going to be** light all night.
>
> You'**re going to meet** me at the airport.　　　My friends **aren't going to go** shopping.
>
> We'**re going to get together** with some of my friends.　　They'**re not going to eat** outside this weekend.

B **Complete the sentences with *be going to* and the affirmative or negative form of the verb in parentheses ( ).**

1 I _____ (be) home tomorrow. I have to work at the office.

2 My parents _____ (take) me to lunch on Saturday. They're busy.

3 My friends and I _____ (go) on a trip to Rio next year. We have our tickets!

4 I _____ (study) a lot next week. I have an important test.

5 My friend _____ (meet) me tonight. She's sick.

C PAIR WORK **Change the sentences in exercise 3B so they're true for you. Then compare with a partner.**

> I'm not going to be home tomorrow. I have to go to college.

D ▶ **Now go to page 138. Look at the grammar chart and do the grammar exercise for 10.1.**

4 SPEAKING

A PAIR WORK **What can you do outside in your city? Make a list.**

> We can eat outside at a lot of restaurants.

> True. And we can watch movies outside.

B PAIR WORK **Make outdoor plans with your partner for next weekend. Then share your plans with the class.**

> Next Saturday, we're going have a picnic in …

10.2 BUT IT'S SUMMER THERE!

1 VOCABULARY: Clothes; seasons

A 🔊 **2.31** Listen and repeat the clothes. Then look at the people in your class. How many of the clothes can you see?

B 🔊 **2.32** PAIR WORK Look at the seasons below. Listen and repeat. What seasons do you have where you live? When are they?

spring

summer

fall

winter

dry season

rainy season

hat

coat

pants

shirt

shorts

dress

skirt

shoes

jeans

sweater

T-shirt

boots

C ▶ Now do the vocabulary exercises for 10.2 on page 149.

2 LANGUAGE IN CONTEXT

A 🔊 **2.33** Read and listen. Sofia and her friend discuss Sofia's trip to St. Petersburg. What clothes do they talk about?

🔊 **2.33 Audio script**

Rena So, are you ready for your trip? What clothes are you going to take?

Sofia Yeah, I am! I'm going to take a big **coat**, and I need to buy a **hat**.

Rena Really? But it's **summer** there!

Sofia Yes, but it's Russia, not Florida! It's not hot in the summer.

Rena True, but it's not *cold*. So, are you going to take **pants** and some **sweaters**?

Sofia Yes, I am. No. I don't know. I usually wear **shorts** in the summer here, but … Oh, I know! I can take my **fall** or **spring** pants.

Rena Good idea. And what are you going to wear on your feet?

Sofia I need some new **shoes**. We're going to walk outside a lot. Or maybe **boots**.

Rena When are you going to leave? I mean, are you *really* ready for this trip?

INSIDER ENGLISH

You can say, *Oh, I know!* when you think of a good idea or an answer to a problem.

Oh, I know! I can take my fall or winter pants.

GLOSSARY

wear (v) have clothes on your body

B **PAIR WORK** What season is it now? What clothes do you usually wear? For ideas, watch Anderson's video.

Are your answers the same as Anderson's?

3 GRAMMAR: Questions with *be going to*

A (Circle) the correct answers. Use the sentences in the grammar box to help you.

1 A *yes/no* question with *be going to* begins with **Am, Is,** or **Are** / **What, Where,** or **When**.

2 For information questions with *be going to*, put the question word **before** / **after** *is, are,* or *am*.

Questions with *be going to*

Yes/no questions

Are you **going to take** some sweaters?   Yes, I **am.** / No, I'**m not.**

Is Sofia **going to see** a friend?   Yes, she **is.** / No, she'**s not.**

Information questions

What are you **going to take?**

When are you **going to leave?**

Where is Sofia **going to go?**

Who are you **going to meet?**

B **Put the words in the correct order to make questions.**

1 are / going to / this weekend? / What / you / do   _____

2 study / Are / tonight? / going to / you   _____

3 have / you / What / for dinner? / are / going to   _____

4 on TV? / going to / are / watch / you / What   _____

5 tomorrow? / go / you / are / Where / going to   _____

6 going to / your / next week? / see / Are / friends / you   _____

C ▶ Now go to page 139. Look at the grammar chart and do the grammar exercise for 10.2.

D **PAIR WORK** Read the Accuracy check box. Then ask and answer the questions in exercise 3B with a partner.

✓ **ACCURACY** CHECK

Do **not** use *be going to* in short answers.
Are you going to wear a dress to the party?
No, I'm not ~~going to.~~ ✗
Yes, I am. ✓

4 SPEAKING

A **Look at the trips. Choose two, and plan what clothes you're going to take with you.**

■ A two-week trip to Miami, Florida, in the summer. (29°C / 84°F)

■ A one-week trip to Vienna, Austria, in the winter. (2°C / 36°F)

■ A five-day trip to Vancouver, Canada, in the spring. (20°C / 68°F)

■ A two-week trip to Manaus, Brazil, in the rainy season. (30°C / 86°F)

B **PAIR WORK** Ask questions about your partners' trips.

Where are you going to go?

First, I'm going to go to Miami this summer.

Oh, great! What clothes are you going to take?

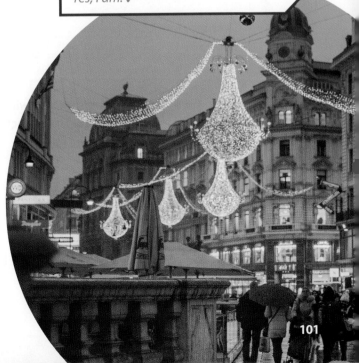

10.3 LET'S MEET AT THE HOTEL

LESSON OBJECTIVE
■ suggest plans for evening activities

1 FUNCTIONAL LANGUAGE

A Jonathan is in Mexico City for a meeting with his coworker, Antonio. They're making plans to go out in the evening. What do you think they are saying?

B ◀)) **2.34** Read and listen. Where are Antonio and Jonathan going to have dinner? Where are they going to meet? What time are they going to meet?

◀)) 2.34 Audio script

Antonio	So, Jonathan, **why don't we go out tonight?**
Jonathan	**OK, sounds good.**
Antonio	Do you like Mexican food?
Jonathan	I love it! Are there any good Mexican restaurants in town?
Antonio	Um, in Mexico City? Yeah, I know one or two places!
Jonathan	I'm sure you do!
Antonio	There's a very good restaurant near your hotel. Why don't we go there?
Jonathan	**Good idea.**
Antonio	So **let's meet at the hotel.**
Jonathan	OK. What time? Eight o'clock?
Antonio	Um … **I'm sorry, but I can't.** How about eight-thirty?
Jonathan	**Yes, sure.**

C Complete the chart with expressions in **bold** from the conversation above.

Making suggestions	Accepting suggestions	Refusing suggestions
1 _____ go out tonight? 2 _____ meet at the hotel.	OK, 3 _____ good. Good 4 _____ . Yes, 5 _____ .	I'm sorry, 6 _____ . Sorry, I'm busy.

D ◀)) **2.35** Complete the conversations with words from exercise 1C. Listen and check. Then practice with a partner.

1 A _____ take a break.
  B OK, sounds _____ .

2 A _____ have lunch?
  B _____ , but I can't.

3 A Coffee?
  B _____ idea.

2 REAL-WORLD STRATEGY

SAYING WHY YOU CAN'T DO SOMETHING
After you say, *I'm sorry, but I can't*, you can give a reason with *I have to*.
Jonathan   *What time? Eight o'clock?*
Antonio   *I'm sorry, but I can't. I have to go home first. How about eight-thirty?*

A   Read the information in the box above. Why can't Antonio meet at eight o'clock?

B   ◀)) 2.36 Listen to a conversation. What are the man and woman going to do, and when?

C   ◀)) 2.36 Listen again. Why can't the woman have a meeting on Monday?

D   ▶ PAIR WORK Student A: Go to page 158. Student B: Go to page 160. Follow the instructions.

3 PRONUNCIATION: Saying the letter *s*

A   ◀)) 2.37 Listen and repeat. How is the letter *s* different in the words?

/s/ **s**orry   /z/ bu**s**y

B   ◀)) 2.38 Read and say the words below. Which sound does the letter *s* have? Write /s/ or /z/. Some words have two sounds. Then listen and check.

1 restaurants   3 tickets   5 station   7 jeans

2 movies   4 shoes   6 season   8 shorts

C   ◀)) 2.39 PAIR WORK Listen and repeat the sentences. Focus on the /s/ and /z/ sounds. Then practice the sentences with a partner.

1 Are there any re**s**taurant**s** in town?   3 Are there any movie**s** on TV tonight?
2 I'm **s**orry, but I can't. I'm bu**s**y tonight.   4 Why don't we get ticket**s** at the **s**tation?

4 SPEAKING

PAIR WORK Imagine your partner is in your town or city on a business or study trip. He/She is staying at a hotel in the city. Suggest something to do in the evening. Also suggest a place to go and a time to meet. Then change roles.

Let's go out this evening.

Good idea.

Why don't we go to a restaurant? Do you like Italian food?

A 24-HOUR CITY

1 LISTENING

A **PAIR WORK** Look at the city in the pictures on pages 104 and 105. What do you think you can you do there?

B ◀)) **2.40** **LISTEN FOR DETAILS** Listen to the start of a TV travel show about Montevideo. Which <u>two</u> cities does the woman talk about? Which <u>two</u> neighborhoods in Montevideo does she talk about?

C ◀)) **2.40** **LISTEN FOR EXAMPLES** Listen again. Check (✓) the places the woman says.

☐ restaurants   ☐ places to go dancing   ☐ hotels
☐ the ocean   ☐ the beach   ☐ museums

D **PAIR WORK** **THINK CRITICALLY** The woman says, "This really is a day-and-night city." Look at the places in exercise 1C. Where do people usually go: in the day? at night? at night *and* in the day?

2 PRONUNCIATION: Listening for *going to*

A ◀)) **2.41** Listen to the sentences. Do you hear *going to* or *gonna*? Circle the correct words.

1 I'm not *going to* / *gonna* go dancing now.

2 We're *going to* / *gonna* walk by the ocean in Old City.

B ◀)) **2.42** Listen. What do you hear? Circle *going to* or *gonna*.

1 *going to* / *gonna*   3 *going to* / *gonna*
2 *going to* / *gonna*   4 *going to* / *gonna*

C People often use *gonna* in informal conversations. Circle the correct answer.

People usually say *gonna* when they are **at work** / **talking to friends**.

3 WRITING

A Read the online invitation. What does Ramon say his friends can wear? Which night is a surprise?

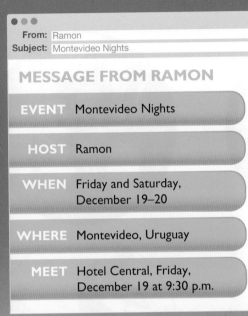

Reply Forward

From: Ramon
Subject: Montevideo Nights

MESSAGE FROM RAMON

EVENT	Montevideo Nights
HOST	Ramon
WHEN	Friday and Saturday, December 19–20
WHERE	Montevideo, Uruguay
MEET	Hotel Central, Friday, December 19 at 9:30 p.m.

This is a city that never sleeps. *You're* not going to sleep, either! ★☺ Meet me at the front door of the hotel. Don't be late! And don't eat dinner first because we're going to eat at a nice restaurant in the Pocitos neighborhood. Then we're going to go dancing – all night! Early in the morning, about 5:00 a.m., we're going to watch the sunrise at the beach and then go for a morning walk by the ocean. It's a great place for a picnic – a breakfast picnic. ☺ And then why don't we play soccer on the beach? A lot of people play soccer on the beach in the summer. You can wear shorts and a T-shirt, but a sweater is good for the early morning. On Saturday night, we're going to … well, it's a surprise! 😮 See you Friday night!

GLOSSARY

sunrise (*n*) early in the morning, when the sun is first in the sky
surprise (*n*) something you don't know about

B **WRITING SKILLS** Look at the contractions in two of Ramon's sentences below. Then <u>underline</u> all 10 contractions in his message. Work with a partner and say the full forms.

<u>You're</u> not going to sleep, either! (*You're = You are*)

<u>Don't</u> be late! (*Don't = Do not*)

REGISTER CHECK

Many speakers of English use contractions in informal writing. In formal writing, people often use the full forms.

 WRITE IT

FIND IT

C Plan an exciting day or night out for your friends. You can look online for ideas. Then write an online invitation. Use Ramon's invitation for an example. Describe where you are going to go and what you are going to do. Use contractions.

D GROUP WORK Read the other invitations in your group. Which events do you want to go to? Why?

10.5

TIME TO SPEAK
48 hours in your city

A **PREPARE** Look at the pictures. Can you do these things in your country? When can you do them? Think about seasons, days, and times of day.

B **RESEARCH** Work with a partner. Choose a season or a month. Think of fun things to do in your city in that season/month during the day, at night, and outside. Write a list.

C **AGREE** Plan a fun weekend (48 hours) in your city. Choose activities from exercise B. Make a plan for Saturday and Sunday.

D **DISCUSS** Work with another pair and compare your plans. Ask and answer questions about their plan.

E **PRESENT** With your partner, present your 48-hour plan to the class. Which plan do you want to do?

To check your progress, go to page 155.

USEFUL PHRASES

RESEARCH
Let's talk about the summer / February / the rainy season.

What fun things can we do during the day? at night? outside?

DISCUSS
We're going to have breakfast in the park.

Are you going to have a picnic?

PRESENT
We're planning a fun weekend in (season/month).

First, we're going to …

On Saturday/Sunday, …

UNIT OBJECTIVES
- describe people, places, and things in the past
- talk about colors and memories
- talk about movies and actors
- write an email about things you keep from your past
- talk about TV shows from your childhood

COLORFUL MEMORIES

11

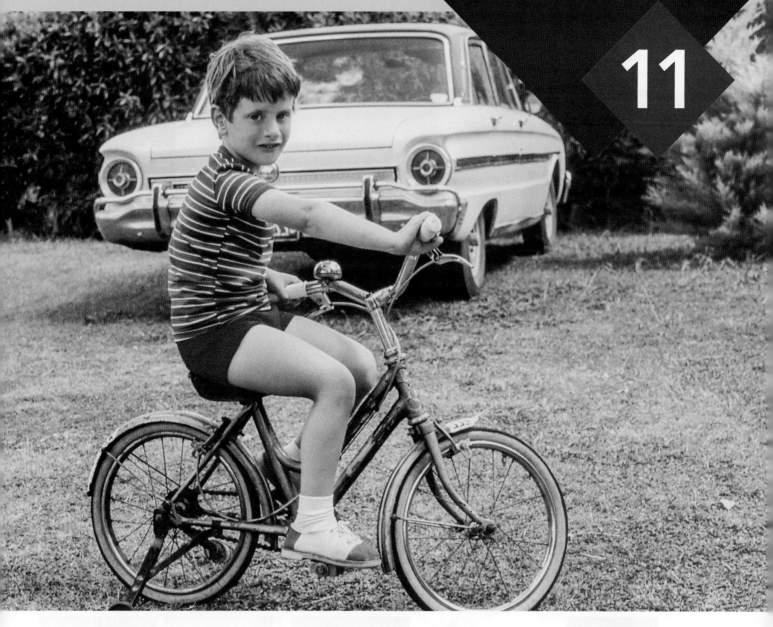

START SPEAKING

A   **Look at the picture. Where is the boy? How old is the boy now?**

B   **Is the boy happy? Why or why not?**

C   **Talk about a happy time in your life. For ideas, watch Felipe's video.**

REAL STUDENT

What time does Felipe talk about? Do you remember the same time?

11.1 FLASHBACK FRIDAY

LESSON OBJECTIVE
■ describe people, places, and things in the past

1 LANGUAGE IN CONTEXT

A Mason writes about two old pictures from his past. Read his posts and the comments. (Circle) the topics he writes about.

his school	his first job
the season	a toy
his family	his favorite food

B Read again. Check (✓) the sentences that are true. Correct the false ones.

☐ 1 Flashback Friday is for pictures from the past.

☐ 2 The yard is at Mason's parents' house.

☐ 3 Bethany is Mason's friend now.

☐ 4 Mason drives a car these days.

2 VOCABULARY: Describing people, places, and things

A 🔊 2.43 Listen and repeat the adjectives in **bold**. Which adjectives in Mason's posts describe people, places, and things?

Mason Clark It's Flashback Friday! Here are two of my favorite memories from 2009. I was eight. This was in the summer. I was with my sister, and we were on vacation at my grandparents' house. My parents weren't there. It was **exciting**! #flashbackfriday #2009 #summervacation

Mason Clark
Bethany Clark

Fay L. Wright You were really **cute**!

Bert Chow Your grandparents' yard was **beautiful**!

Mason Clark Yeah, it was **wonderful**. It was usually **quiet**, but not in the summer. We were **noisy** kids!

Mason Clark And this was my old go-kart. My grandpa made it for me. Well, it wasn't old in 2009 – it was **new** then! It was **slow**, but to me, at eight, it was really **fast** and exciting. #go-kart #2009 #bestgrandparents

Sam Lopez My go-kart was **awful**, but yours is great.

Bethany Clark Hey, Mason is still driving it today! 😄

Mason Clark Don't listen to my sister! I have a real, *fast* car now. 🙂

👍 13 ❤ 2

GLOSSARY

memories (*n*) things you think about from your past
yard (*n*) the outdoor area in front of or behind a house

new shoes

cute dog

wonderful vacation

noisy baby

fast car

 — exciting book / beautiful day / awful day / quiet baby / slow car

exciting book

beautiful day

awful day

quiet baby

slow car

B ▶ Now do the vocabulary exercises for 11.1 on page 150.

C GROUP WORK Think about a person, place, or thing from your past. Describe it to your group. Use the adjectives in exercise 2A. For ideas, watch Anderson's video.

REAL STUDENT

Is Anderson's memory happy? Is your memory happy, too?

3 GRAMMAR: Statements with *was* and *were*

A (Circle) **the correct answer. Use the sentences in the grammar box to help you.**

1 Use *was* and *were* to talk about people, places, or things in the **past** / **future**.

2 *Was* and *were* are the simple past forms of **go** / **be**.

3 *Was* and *were* are **affirmative** / **negative**.

4 *Wasn't* and *weren't* are **affirmative** / **negative**.

Statements with *was* and *were*

I **was** in the yard.	My parents **weren't** there.
We **were** on vacation.	It **wasn't** old.

B **Read another Flashback Friday post. Complete the post with *was*, *wasn't*, *were*, or *weren't*.**

Ethan Collins
March 14 at 3:37 p.m.

I remember a visit to my uncle's farm in August 1998. It ¹ _____ a big farm – just a nice, small one. There ² _____ a lot of animals, only ten or fifteen. They ³ _____ farm animals, not pets, so they ⁴ _____ friendly, but my uncle's dog ⁵ _____ really nice. He ⁶ _____ only two or three, so he ⁷ _____ very old, but he ⁸ _____ smart. His real name ⁹ _____ Jake, but my name for him ¹⁰ _____ "Fluffy Duffy." It's an awful name, but I ¹¹ _____ seven at the time, and to me, Fluffy Duffy ¹² _____ a beautiful name! We ¹³ _____ great friends.
#flashbackfriday #1998 #bestfriend

👍 Like   💬 Comment   ➤ Share

👍 35   ♥ 8

Fluffy Duffy

GLOSSARY
remember (*v*) think about something from the past

C ▶ **Now go to page 139. Look at the grammar chart and do the grammar exercise for 11.1.**

D PAIR WORK **Write sentences with *was* or *were*. Use the words in parentheses ( ). Then check your accuracy. Which sentences are true for you?**

When I was a child …

1 (My friends / wonderful) _____ .

2 (My hometown / beautiful) _____ .

3 (My brother's car / awful) _____ .

4 (My cat / really cute) _____ .

✓ **ACCURACY** CHECK

Do **not** forget to use *was, wasn't, were,* or *weren't* before adjectives when describing the past.

He cute. ✗
He was cute. ✓

4 SPEAKING

A **Choose one or two of your memories. Think about the ideas below or your own ideas. Write notes.**

ages	animals	the people	the place	the season	the year	things

B PAIR WORK **Talk about your memories. You can begin, *"I remember …"***

I remember my sister's birthday party. It was July 2006. She was thirteen. The party was very noisy, and …

11.2 OUR OLD PHONE WAS WHITE

1 LANGUAGE IN CONTEXT

A **PAIR WORK** Look at the picture of the child. Describe it with one word.

B 🔊 **2.44** Emilio talks to his wife, Paula. Read and listen. Where was Emilio in the picture? Which rooms does Paula remember?

🔊 **2.44 Audio script**

Emilio Here's another picture of me.

Paula Cute! How old were you?

Emilio I don't know. Two?

Paula And where were you? Were you at home?

Emilio No, I wasn't, because our phone was **black**. Hmm … so where was the **green** phone? Oh, yeah! It was at my grandparents' house, in the kitchen.

Paula Hey, I remember our old phone, too. It was **white**.

Emilio Wow, you remember the color, too! Was it big? Our old phone was *really* big.

Paula Yeah, it was. I remember a lot! The phone was in the living room, next to the couch. The couch was **brown**. And the living room walls were **orange**. Oh, yeah, and my bedroom walls were **pink** and green. Yuck! It's really easy to remember the colors of things – even ugly colors!

GLOSSARY
ugly (*adj*) not nice to look at

C 🔊 **2.44** Read and listen again. Then answer the questions.

1 How many phones does Emilio talk about?
2 Paula remembers the color of her phone, living room walls, bedroom walls – and which other thing?

2 VOCABULARY: Colors

A 🔊 **2.45** **PAIR WORK** Listen and repeat the colors. Which colors are in the conversation above? What's your favorite color?

INSIDER ENGLISH

You can say, *Oh, yeah,* when you remember something.

Where was the green phone? **Oh, yeah!** *It was at my grandmother's house.*

Oh, yeah, *and my bedroom walls were pink and green.*

---

white | gray | red | yellow | purple | brown
black | blue | green | orange | pink

B ▶ Now do the vocabulary exercises for 11.2 on page 150.

C **PAIR WORK** Tell your partner the colors of <u>two</u> things from your home.

3 GRAMMAR: Questions with *was* and *were*

A (Circle) the correct answers. Use the questions in the grammar box to help you.

1 In *yes/no* questions, *was* and *were* go at the **beginning** / **end** of the question.

2 In information questions, *was* and *were* go **before** / **after** the question word(s) (for example, *How old* and *When*).

> **Questions with *was* and *were***
>
> | *Yes/no* questions | Information questions |
> |---|---|
> | **Were** you at home? | How old **were** you? |
> | No, I **wasn't**. | I **was** two. |
> | **Was** the phone in the kitchen? | What color **were** the walls? |
> | Yes, it **was**. | They **were** orange. |

B | PAIR WORK | **Put the words in the correct order to make questions. Then ask and answer the questions with a partner.**

1 color / your old phone? / was / What _____

2 was / the phone? / Where _____

3 in the kitchen? / the refrigerator / Was _____

4 the walls / color / in the kitchen? / were / What _____

5 big? / Were / the bedrooms _____

6 your home / nice? / Was _____

C ▶ Now go to page 140. Look at the grammar chart and do the grammar exercise for 11.2.

4 SPEAKING

A **Draw a picture or plan of a room in your house from your past. Include furniture and your favorite things.**

B | PAIR WORK | **Work with a partner. Ask and answer questions about your rooms.**

> This is the bedroom. There was a bed, a desk, and two windows.

> What color was the bed?

> My bed was white.

111

11.3 I HAVE NO IDEA

1 FUNCTIONAL LANGUAGE

A Look at the picture of the woman. Do you know her name? What else do you know about her?

B 🔊 **2.46** Read and listen. What does the man want to remember? Does he remember it?

🔊 2.46 Audio script

A I'm going to watch *Titanic* tonight.

B The movie?

A Yeah. With Leonardo DiCaprio, and … who was the other actor? The woman?

B Um, **I have no idea.**

A She's from England.

B Sorry, **I'm not sure.**

A Her first name is Kate, **I think.**

B Let me think. **Maybe** it's Kate Hudson? No, she's American. Why don't we look online?

A Good idea. Let's see … *Titanic* actor, woman … Kate Winslet!

B Oh, yeah.

A What was the name of that other movie she was in? With Johnny Depp.

B Oh no … Not again!

GLOSSARY
actor (*n*) a man or woman in a movie, TV show, or play

C Complete the chart with expressions in **bold** from the conversation above.

Expressing uncertainty	
Very unsure	**A little unsure**
I have ¹_____.	Her first name is Kate, I ³_____.
I'm ²_____.	I think her first name is Kate.
I don't know.	⁴_____ it's Kate Hudson?

D 🔊 **2.47** [PAIR WORK] Complete the conversations with the correct words from the box. Listen and check. Then practice with a partner.

> don't   Maybe   no   not   think

1 A When was the movie *Titanic* in theaters?

   B I _____ know. _____ it was in 1997?

2 A How many movies was Kate Winslet in?

   B I have _____ idea.

3 A Where was Melinda yesterday?

   B I _____ she was at home.

4 A Where are the restrooms?

   B Sorry, I'm _____ sure.

2 REAL-WORLD STRATEGY

TAKING TIME TO THINK

When you need time to think about an answer, say, *Let me think*, *Uh*, or *Um*.

Um, I have no idea.

Let me think. Maybe it's Kate Hudson?

A   Read the information in the box about taking time to think. Which <u>two</u> expressions does the woman use?

B   ◄)) **2.48** Listen to a conversation. What is the man sure about? What <u>isn't</u> he sure about?

C   ◄)) **2.48** Listen again. Which <u>two</u> expressions does the man use when he needs time to think?

D   ▶   PAIR WORK   Student A: Go to page 158. Student B: Go to page 160. Follow the instructions.

3 PRONUNCIATION: Saying /oʊ/ and /ɑː/ vowel sounds

A   ◄)) **2.49** Listen and repeat the words. How are the vowel sounds different?

/oʊ/   know   /ɑː/   not

B   ◄)) **2.50** Listen. Write A for words with /oʊ/, for example *know*. Write B for words with /ɑː/, for example *not*.

1 don't ___		**3** no ___		**5** home ___	
2 on ___		**4** go ___		**6** concert ___	

C   ◄)) **2.51**   PAIR WORK   Look at the letters in **bold** below. Listen and repeat. Then practice the conversations with a partner.

1   **A**   Was M**o**na at the c**o**ncert yesterday?
    B   N**o**, she wasn't. She was at h**o**me.

2   **A**   Where is Leonard**o** DiCapri**o** from?
    B   I have n**o** idea.

3   **A**   D**o**n't g**o**!
    B   Sorry, I have to g**o** h**o**me.

4   **A**   Are we **o**n the right bus? It's very sl**ow**.
    B   I d**o**n't know.

4 SPEAKING

GROUP WORK   Think of a movie. Ask other people in your group about the actors in it. Then change roles.

> Who was in the first *Avatar*?

> I have no idea.

> Um, was Zoe Saldana in it?

> Yes, she was.

THINGS WE KEEP

1 READING

A Look at the pictures. What things can you see? Are the things old or new? Do you have some of these things?

B READ FOR MAIN IDEAS Read the article. What is it about?

PICTURING MEMORIES

Terry Lawrence is a travel writer for Pak Airlines in-flight magazine. Today she takes a break from travel writing and tells Pak Airlines readers about what she does in her free time.

I love to travel, I love to write – and I love to take pictures! I often take pictures of people and their favorite things. I have hundreds of pictures of people and the things they keep. People around the world keep things from childhood, for example toy cars, books, and games. These were their first favorite things. And me? I like to keep photographs, of course! Here are some of my favorite pictures.

Meet Tom Bradley and his toy cars. They were birthday gifts. They're old, but he plays with them today – with a little help!

Many parents keep their children's things, like baby shoes or a child's first clothes. Rosa Ortiz keeps her daughter's shoe and her son's shoe in her car. They were one and two years old at the time. Now they're 12 and 13!

Many people keep books and comic books. This is Doug and one of his comic books, but it's not his favorite. Doug leaves his favorite comic book at home – it's very expensive!

GLOSSARY
childhood (*n*) the time when you were a child
keep (*v*) have something for a long time

C READ FOR DETAIL Read again. Then read these sentences from the article. What do the underlined words mean? (Circle) the answers.

1 These were their first favorite things.
    These =   **a** children   **b** birthday gifts   **c** things from their childhood
2 They're old, but he plays with them today.
    They and *them* =   **a** toy cars   **b** shoes   **c** games
3 They were one and two years old at the time.
    They =   **a** Rosa's cars   **b** Rosa's parents   **c** Rosa's children
4 It's not his favorite.
    It =   **a** Doug   **b** Doug's comic book   **c** Doug's house

D PAIR WORK What things do you keep? Why? Do you keep the same things from the article, too? Tell a partner.

2 WRITING

A **Read Angie's email to her brother. What things from the past does she find in a box?**

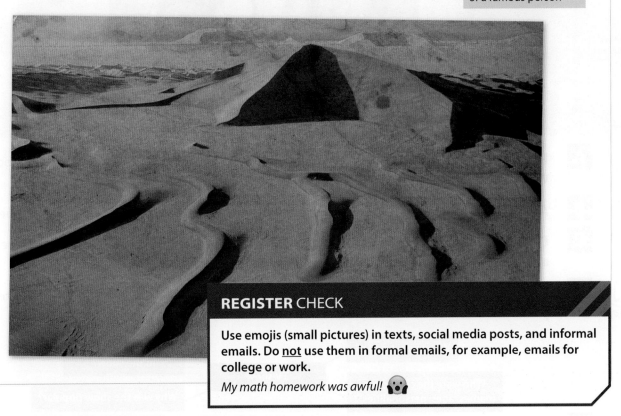

Reply Forward

Hi Eddie,

Do you remember this postcard? It was in a box under my bed. It was from Grandpa Bowman in 1969. He was in Saudi Arabia. His postcards were always exciting, and this one was my favorite. The desert is really beautiful. Do *you* have any of his old postcards?

There was also a lot of homework from my school days in the box. Hey, I was smart! Well, usually. My math homework was awful! 😱 I don't think I want to keep it.

Your old soccer ball was in the box, too. ⚽ Why do I have it? I don't know. There's some writing on it. Maybe it's the autograph of a famous soccer player. Do you want it?

Love,

Angie

GLOSSARY

autograph (*n*) name in handwriting, usually of a famous person

REGISTER CHECK

Use emojis (small pictures) in texts, social media posts, and informal emails. Do **not** use them in formal emails, for example, emails for college or work.

My math homework was awful! 😱

B PAIR WORK THINK CRITICALLY **Why does Angie's email have three paragraphs?**

C WRITING SKILLS **Read the topic sentence from the email below. The topic sentence tells you what the paragraph is about. Read the email again and <u>underline</u> the three topic sentences.**

Do you remember this postcard? (= this paragraph is about a postcard.)

 WRITE IT

D **Imagine you have a box of old things from your childhood. Write an email to a friend about <u>two</u> or <u>three</u> things in the box. Use a new paragraph for each thing. Write a topic sentence for each paragraph. You can use emojis.**

E PAIR WORK **Read your partner's email. What interesting things do they write about in their email?**

11.5 TIME TO SPEAK
TV memories

A **PREPARE** Work with a partner. Talk about old TV shows you remember from your childhood. Write notes.

B **AGREE** Compare your ideas with other students. Which shows do a lot of people remember?

C **DISCUSS** Choose a TV show from your conversations in exercise A or B. What do you remember about it? Talk about the names, places, and things in the show.

D **PREPARE** Prepare a presentation about your TV show from exercise C. Include the ideas below and your own ideas. You can go online and find information you don't remember.

FIND IT

When was it on TV?

Who were the characters (names, ages, personalities)?

TV show

What were the places in the show?

Why was the show popular?

E **PRESENT** Present your memories of the TV show to the class with your partner. Which shows does everyone remember?

To check your progress, go to page 155.

USEFUL PHRASES

DISCUSS
I remember … from my childhood.
What about you?
Let's talk about the characters in …
What were their names?
I liked that show because …

AGREE
What do you remember?
A lot of people / I remember …

PRESENT
We're talking about …
Our show was really popular.
It was on TV in (year).

UNIT OBJECTIVES
■ talk about snacks and small meals
■ talk about meals in restaurants
■ offer and accept food and drink
■ write a restaurant review
■ create a menu for a restaurant

STOP, EAT, GO

12

START SPEAKING

A   Which meal do you think these men are eating: breakfast, lunch, or dinner? Is it a big meal or a small meal? Are they enjoying their food?

B   For a good meal, you need good food – and what else? Do you see these things in the picture?

C   Talk about a good meal you remember. You can talk about where and when it was, who you were with, and why it was good.

BACKPACKING AND SNACKING

LESSON OBJECTIVE
■ talk about snacks and small meals

1 VOCABULARY: Snacks and small meals

A 🔊 **2.52** [PAIR WORK] **Listen and repeat. Then choose something you want to eat now.**

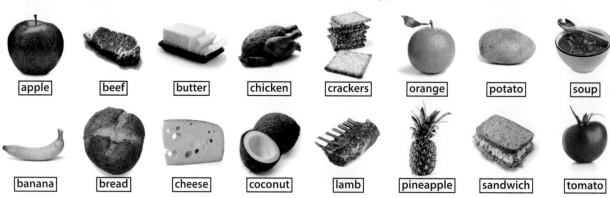

apple | beef | butter | chicken | crackers | orange | potato | soup

banana | bread | cheese | coconut | lamb | pineapple | sandwich | tomato

> **!** To make these words plural, add -*s* or -*es*:
>
> *banana* → *bananas*   *tomato* → *tomatoes*   *sandwich* → *sandwiches*
>
> Some nouns are non-count, for example *cheese* and *soup*.

B ▶ **Now do the vocabulary exercises for 12.1 on page 151.**

C [PAIR WORK] **Look at the pictures in exercise 1A and find:**

- <u>seven</u> words for fruit and vegetables
- <u>three</u> words for meat
- <u>two</u> words for dairy products
- <u>two</u> words for grain products
- <u>two</u> words for small meals

2 LANGUAGE IN CONTEXT

A **Read the blog. Where was Tyler yesterday? Where was he last week?**

B **Read again. Check (✓) the sentences that are true. Correct the false ones.**

☐ 1 Tyler's breakfast and lunch were big.

☐ 2 There was meat in Tyler's sandwich.

☐ 3 There were dairy products in Tyler's breakfast, lunch, and dinner.

☐ 4 There are dairy products and fruit in *locro*.

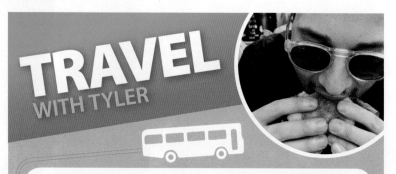

TRAVEL
WITH TYLER

Hello from Salvador, Brazil! I'm happy to be here after a really long trip. Yesterday, I took the bus from Aracaju. I didn't eat a lot for breakfast before the trip – just some **bread** and **butter**. Then I was on the bus for seven hours. We stopped in a lot of places, but I stayed on the bus, so I didn't have a big lunch. I ate some **crackers** and a **banana**, and I drank a bottle of warm water (yuck!)

I arrived in Salvador in the afternoon, and I was *really* hungry, so I didn't wait. I had dinner at the bus station! I went to a food stand, and I bought a *bauru* **sandwich**. It's bread with **beef**, **cheese**, and **tomatoes**. I needed it! And I liked it – I'm going to eat it again tomorrow.

South American food is great. Last week, in Quito, Ecuador, I tried *locro*. It's a **soup** with **potatoes** and cheese. I love the fruit in South America, too, but because I'm "backpacking and snacking," it's not always easy to eat. You can't eat **pineapples** and **coconuts** on a bus!

GLOSSARY

food stand (*n*) a place to buy food on the street

hungry (*adj*) you need to eat

3 GRAMMAR: Simple past statements

A **Circle** the correct answers. Use the sentences in the grammar box to help you.

1 Use the simple past to talk about **finished events** / **events that are happening now**.

2 After *I*, *you*, *he*, *she*, *we*, *they* and *it*, simple past verbs have **the same** / **different** spelling.

3 Simple past verbs can be regular or irregular. To make most regular past simple verbs, add **-d or -ed** / **-s**.

4 To make negative statements in the simple past, use **don't** / **didn't** + verb (for example, *eat*, *drink*, or *have*).

Simple past statements

Yesterday, I **took** the bus from Aracaju.

I **had** some soup. He **had** a big dinner.

She **wanted** an orange. We **wanted** some apples.

I **didn't eat** a lot for breakfast.

She **didn't like** the sandwich.

They **didn't drink** the coffee.

! Irregular past simple verbs do not end in *-ed*. For example, *I took the bus*, <u>not</u> *I ~~taked~~ the bus*.

eat → ate   drink → drank   have → had   go → went   take → took   buy → bought

For more irregular verbs, go to page 161.

B Read the information about irregular verbs in the Notice box. Then (circle) the correct words.

1 It was a really big sandwich, but I *ate / eat* it all.

2 We *have / had* fish for dinner last night.

3 She didn't *buy / bought* food at the supermarket.

4 I was hungry and really *needed / need* some food.

5 We *arrive / arrived* at the restaurant at 5:30, but it wasn't open.

6 Was the cheese good? I didn't *tried / try* it.

C ▶ Now go to page 140. Look at the grammar charts and do the grammar exercise for 12.1.

D [PAIR WORK] Complete the sentences so they're true for you. Then compare with a partner.

1 For breakfast, I ate _____ , and I drank _____ .

2 Last week, I bought _____ at the supermarket.

3 The last movie I watched was _____ .

4 Last weekend, I went to _____ with _____ .

4 SPEAKING

A [PAIR WORK] Talk about the food in exercise 1A. Say which things you like and which you <u>don't</u> like. For ideas, watch June's video.

REAL STUDENT

Do you like/not like the same things as June?

B [PAIR WORK] Give examples of snacks and small meals you ate last week. Ask your partner questions about what they ate.

Yesterday, I ate a sandwich for lunch.

Was it good?

1 VOCABULARY: Food, drinks, and desserts

A ◀)) **2.53** Look at the pictures. Listen and repeat.

B **PAIR WORK** Which things in exercise 1A are drinks? Which are desserts? Which ones do you like? Which <u>don't</u> you like?

C ▶ Now do the vocabulary exercises for 12.2 on page 151.

D **GROUP WORK** What do you usually eat and drink for breakfast, lunch, and dinner? Tell your group. For ideas, watch Anderson's video.

REAL STUDENT

What's Anderson's food routine? Is your routine the same or different?

rice

steak
eggs

black beans

pizza   soda

fish
green beans

ice cream
chocolate cake

juice
water

2 LANGUAGE IN CONTEXT

A ◀)) **2.54** Jackie and Yoo-ri are writing comments on a restaurant review card. Read and listen. Did they like their meal?

B ◀)) **2.54** Read and listen again. What did Jackie and Yoo-ri eat? What did they drink?

◀)) **2.54 Audio script**

Jackie	Look, a comment card. Let's do it.
Yoo-ri	OK. We have time before dessert.
Jackie	Number one. "What did you eat?" You had **fish** and **rice**. Did you have any vegetables?
Yoo-ri	Yeah. I had beans, **black beans**.
Jackie	That's right. And I had the **steak** with potatoes and **green beans**. OK. Number 2. "What did you drink?" I just had **water**. Did you have apple **juice**?
Yoo-ri	No, I didn't have any juice. I had a **soda**.
Jackie	Oh, yeah. OK, number 3. "How was the food?" My steak was great, but I didn't like the potatoes. The green beans were OK. Did you like the fish?
Yoo-ri	Yes, I did. It was wonderful, and the rice and beans were good, too. But my soda was warm.
Jackie	Hmm … I'm going to check "good." Ah, the server is coming with dessert. Oh, wow! Look at our **chocolate cake** and **ice cream**.
Yoo-ri	Yum! Change "good" to "great!"

☕ *Clinton Street Restaurant*
201 Clinton Street 📞 219–555–2310

Tell us what you think!

Name(s): ___Jackie___ and ___Yoo-ri___
1 What did you eat? _____
2 What did you drink? _____
3 How was the food?
   ○ great   ○ good   ○ OK   ○ awful
4 Were you happy with your server? ○ yes   ○ no
5 How did you hear about us?
   ○ a friend   ○ online   ○ walking by   ○ other

INSIDER ENGLISH

Some people use *waiter* for a man and *waitress* for a woman. But these days, many people use the word *server* for a man or a woman.

3 GRAMMAR: Simple past questions; *any*

A **Circle the correct answers. Use the information in the grammar box and the Notice box to help you.**

1 In simple past *yes/no* questions, use **Did / Do** + verb.

2 In simple past information questions, the question word and *did* go **before / after** the person or thing.

3 You can use *any* with **yes/no / information** questions in the simple past.

Simple past questions	
Yes/no questions	**Information questions**
Did you **have** apple juice?	**How did** you **hear** about us?
Did she **like** the fish?	**What** did they **eat**?
Did they **eat** any ice cream?	

> **!** Use *some* in affirmative statements. Use *any* in yes/no questions and negative statements.
> *I had **some** soup for lunch.*
> *Did you have **any** dessert?*
> *They didn't have **any** juice.*

B **PAIR WORK** **Complete the conversations with the simple past form of the verbs in parentheses ( ). Then practice with a partner and make the answers true for you.**

1 A _____ you _____ (eat) breakfast?

 B Yes, I _____ .

2 A What _____ you _____ (have) for lunch?

 B I _____ an egg sandwich.

3 A _____ your friends _____ (go out) for dinner last night?

 B No, they _____ .

4 A What _____ your sisters _____ (buy) at the mall?

 B They _____ some shoes. They _____ any lunch.

5 A _____ your teacher _____ (give) you any homework?

 B No, she _____ .

C ▶ Now go to page 141. Look at the grammar charts and do the grammar exercise for 12.2.

D **PAIR WORK** **Write questions with these words. Use your ideas for the words in parentheses ( ). Then ask and answer the questions with a partner.**

> what / do / (time or day)   have (food item) / for (meal) / yesterday   where / go / (time or day)

4 SPEAKING

A **PAIR WORK** **You're going to ask your partner about a meal they had in a restaurant. Ask the questions from the comment card and the box below. Then think of two more questions.**

> Where did you eat?   Was the food expensive?
> Did you have any dessert?   Was the restaurant busy?
> Did you wait for a table?   Who did you eat with?

B **PAIR WORK** **Ask and answer the questions from exercise 4A about a meal you ate last week or a favorite meal you had in the past.**

> Where did you eat?

> I had dinner at The Fish Dish.

☕ Clinton Street Restaurant
201 Clinton Street   ▯ 219–555–2310

Tell us what you think!

Name(s): _____ and _____

1 What did you eat? _____

2 What did you drink? _____

3 How was the food?
   ○ great   ○ good   ○ OK   ○ awful

4 Were you happy with your server?   ○ yes   ○ no

5 How did you hear about us?
   ○ a friend   ○ online   ○ walking by   ○ other

12.3 PLEASE PASS THE BUTTER

1 FUNCTIONAL LANGUAGE

A 🔊 **2.55** Elisa has dinner in two different places on different nights. Read and listen to two conversations. What food and drink does Elisa want? What doesn't she want?

🔊 **2.55 Audio script**

1
Elisa	I really like this fish, Dan. It's so good!
Dan	Thanks. **Do you want** some more?
Elisa	Yes, please. Thanks. **Can I have** some bread, please?
Dan	**Of course.** Here. **Would you like** some potatoes?
Elisa	No, thanks, but **please pass** the butter.
Dan	OK. **Here you are.**

2
Server	**What would you like to eat?**
Elisa	**I'd like** the chicken and rice, please.
Server	**All right.** And what would you like to drink?
Elisa	**Do you have** iced tea?
Server	Yes. **We have** small and large iced teas.
Elisa	I'd like a large iced tea, please. It's so hot today!

B Complete the chart with expressions in **bold** from the conversations above. Then read the information in the Accuracy check box. What food does Elisa request with *some*?

Offering food and drink	Requesting food and drink
1 _____ some more?	4 _____ some bread, please?
2 _____ some potatoes?	5 _____ the butter.
3 _____ to eat? / to drink?	6 _____ the chicken and rice, please.
What would you like for dessert?	7 _____ iced tea?

Responding to requests
Of 8 _____ .
Here. / Here 9 _____ .
All 10 _____ . / OK.
11 _____ small and large iced teas.

GLOSSARY
more (*det*) another piece (of fish, for example)
iced tea (*n*) cold tea

✓ ACCURACY CHECK

Use *any* in questions.
Did you have any vegetables?

You can use *some* when a question is a request.
Can I have ~~any~~ bread? ✗
Can I have some bread? ✓

C 🔊 **2.56** [PAIR WORK] Put the two conversations in the correct order. Listen and check. Then practice with a partner.

1
___ Yes, please. It's good!
___ OK. Here you are.
___ Would you like some more chicken?
___ And please pass the potatoes.

2
___ No, sorry.
___ What would you like for dessert?
___ I see. OK, I'd like ice cream and coffee, please.
___ Let me think. Do you have any chocolate cake?

2 REAL-WORLD STRATEGY

USING *SO* AND *REALLY* TO MAKE WORDS STRONGER

Use *so* before adjectives to make them stronger. Use *really* before some verbs to make them stronger, for example: *like, love, don't like, need (to), want (to), have to.*

Elisa   *I really like this fish, Dan. It's so good!*

Elisa   *I'd like a large iced tea. It's so hot today!*

A   **Read the information in the box above about making words stronger. What adjectives does Elisa use with *so*? What verb does she use with *really*?**

B   ◀)) **2.57** **Listen to a conversation. What does the man ask for?**

C   ◀)) **2.57** **Listen again. What words does he use after *so* and *really*?**

3 PRONUNCIATION: Saying /h/ and /r/ sounds

A   ◀)) **2.58** **Listen and repeat the words. Focus on the /h/ and /r/ sounds. How are they different?**

    /h/ have   /r/ really

B   ◀)) **2.59** **Listen. What sound do you hear? Write /h/ or /r/.**

1	___ ear	3	___ ight	5	___ appy	7	___ ad
2	___ ave	4	___ ead	6	___ ice	8	___ ed

C   ◀)) **2.60** **PAIR WORK** **Listen. Then practice the conversations with a partner. Does your partner say /h/ and /r/ clearly?**

1 **A** How is your food?
    B It's good. I really like this rice.

2 **A** Where did you go last night?
    B We had dinner at The Happy Home restaurant.

3 **A** How did you hear about us?
    B I had an email from a friend. He really likes the food here.

4 SPEAKING

A   **PAIR WORK** **Have a conversation. Use exercise 1C for an example. Choose <u>one</u> of these situations:**

- You're at a friend's home. One person offers food. The other person asks for things.
- You're at a restaurant. One person is a server. The other person orders a meal.
- You're at a café. One person is a server. The other person orders a drink and a snack.

> Would you like some chicken, Matias?

> Yes, please.

B   **GROUP WORK** **Have your conversation again, in front of another pair. Listen. What situation in exercise 4A is it? What food and drink do they talk about?**

12.4 WHAT DID THE REVIEWERS SAY?

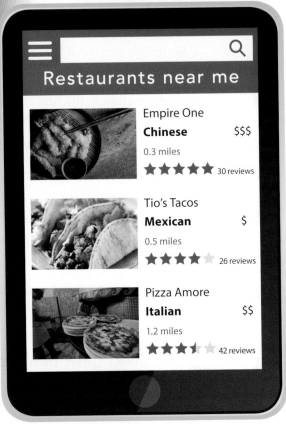

Restaurants near me

Empire One
Chinese $$$
0.3 miles
★★★★★ 30 reviews

Tio's Tacos
Mexican $
0.5 miles
★★★★☆ 26 reviews

Pizza Amore
Italian $$
1.2 miles
★★★☆☆ 42 reviews

1 LISTENING

A Look at the pictures. What are the people doing? Do you use similar apps?

B 🔊 2.61 **LISTEN FOR DETAILS** Listen to the conversation. What food does Mara want to eat?

C 🔊 2.61 **LISTEN FOR SUPPORTING DETAILS** (Circle) the reasons for each statement. Sometimes, there is more than one answer.

1 Eric wants to eat at a restaurant near where they are.

   a He likes to eat in the car.   **b** His favorite restaurants are in the area.   **c** He's hungry.

2 Mara and Eric don't go to Fish Around.

   a Mara doesn't like fish.   **b** Mara ate there in the past.   **c** Eric had a bad meal there.

3 They don't go to Kayla B's Kitchen.

   a The food was bad.   **b** It took a long time to get food.   **c** The restaurant isn't new.

4 They go to Tio's Tacos.

   a It has good reviews.   **b** Mara had a good meal there before.   **c** It's Eric's favorite restaurant.

2 PRONUNCIATION: Listening for *Do you want to … ?*

A 🔊 2.62 Listen and repeat. Focus on the <u>underlined</u> words. How is the pronunciation different than the written words?

1 Where <u>do you want to</u> eat?   2 <u>Do you want</u> Chinese, Mexican, or Italian food?

B 🔊 2.63 Listen to three speakers. How do they say *want to*? Match the speaker (1–3) with the pronunciation (a–c).

  a wanna ___   **b** /dʒu/ want ___   **c** /dʒu/ wanna ___

3 WRITING

A Read two reviews of the restaurant Fish Around. What did Frank and Julieta eat? What was their favorite thing?

Fish Around
Los Angeles, United States

$$ Fish   ★★★★☆ 98 reviews

Frank B. ★★★★★
Los Angeles, USA This is a nice restaurant. It's big, and it has a lot of windows, so it's very light. There are some tall plants in the dining area, but it isn't a "forest." I had vegetable soup, fish, and rice. The soup was good. I love fish, and the fish was great! My brother had fish and vegetables, and he liked his meal, too. We both had dessert. He had cake and I had ice cream. The servers were so friendly. We were really happy with our meal, and it wasn't expensive.

Julieta F. ★★★★★
Buenos Aires, **Argentina** I think this is a good restaurant, but I didn't choose it. My friends like fish, so they wanted to eat here. I like meat, but there wasn't any meat on the menu. Was the food good? Well, my friends liked it. They had fish, vegetables, rice, and dessert. I had fish and potatoes. The potatoes were OK. The fish was … well, it was fish! For dessert, I had pineapple cake and coconut ice cream. Wow! It was so good! I'm giving this restaurant three stars because the dessert was so great. The servers were nice. The price was OK – not cheap, but not expensive.

B **PAIR WORK** **THINK CRITICALLY** **Did Frank and Julieta like their meals? Why or why not?**

C **Read the sentences from the reviews. <u>Underline</u> the things the people ate.**

My brother had fish and vegetables.

I had vegetable soup, fish, and rice.

REGISTER CHECK

In informal writing, you can sometimes ask and answer your own questions.

Was the food good? Well, my friends liked it.

D **WRITING SKILLS** **Read the rules about writing lists, below. (Circle) the correct answers. Use the sentences in exercise 3C to help you. Then <u>underline</u> all the lists of food in the reviews.**

1 To list <u>two</u> things, you can join them with *and*. **Do / don't** use a comma (,) between two things.

2 To list <u>three or more</u> things, you can use a comma (,) between the things. Use *and* **before / after** the last thing.

⊙ WRITE IT

E **Write a review of a restaurant you like. You can write about:**
- the restaurant's appearance
- the food you ate
- your opinion about the food
- your opinion about the servers
- the price of the food

F **GROUP WORK** **Read other people's reviews. Would you like to eat at any of the restaurants?**

12.5 TIME TO SPEAK
Recipe for a great restaurant

A **DISCUSS** Talk about a great restaurant you went to, and say why you liked it. Then talk about a bad restaurant, and say why you <u>didn't</u> like it.

B **PREPARE** Talk about what makes a great restaurant. Think about the things you discussed in exercise A and the things below. Then compare your ideas with other people.

- pizza
- cookies
- Food
- juice
- Location
- Great restaurants!
- Prices
- Furniture
- Servers

FIND IT

C **DECIDE** Work with a partner. Imagine you're opening a new restaurant. Choose a name for your restaurant and talk about the food and drink it has. Then create a great menu. You can go online to find ideas.

D **ROLE PLAY** Work with another pair. Welcome them to your restaurant. They choose a meal from your menu. Then change roles. Continue with other pairs.

E **PRESENT** Tell the class about some of the menus in exercise D. Were they good? What did you choose? What's your favorite menu?

To check your progress, go to page 155.

USEFUL PHRASES

DECIDE
OK. First, what's the name of our restaurant?
What kind of food do we have?
Let's plan a great menu. We can have …

ROLE PLAY
Welcome to our restaurant!
What would you like to eat/drink?
Do you have … ?
So, you would like …

PRESENT
We went to a great restaurant. Its name was …
We liked / didn't like …
Our favorite menu is … because …

REVIEW 4 (UNITS 10–12)

1 VOCABULARY

A Look at the groups of words (1–6). For each group, (circle) the word that does not belong. Then match the groups with the categories (a–d). Some groups match the same category.

1	cheese	fish	potato	chicken	coat	___		
2	white	winter	rainy season	summer	dry season	___	a	colors
3	red	green	brown	fall	yellow	___	b	clothes
4	shirt	dress	skirt	pants	rice	___	c	food
5	purple	blue	shorts	gray	black	___	d	seasons
6	banana	tomato	apple	pink	cake	___		

B Match each word you (circled) in 1–6 to a different category (a–d). Then add <u>one</u> extra word to the categories.

2 GRAMMAR

A Make questions and answers in the simple past. Use the words in parentheses ( ).

1 A _____ you _____ a good weekend? (have)

   B Yes, it _____ great, thanks. (be)

2 A What _____ you _____? (eat)

   B We _____ some Japanese food. (try)

3 A Where _____ you on Saturday? (be)

   B I _____ at home in the morning, but not in the afternoon. (be)

4 A What _____ you _____ on TV last night? (watch)

   B A movie, but it _____ very good. (not be)

5 A _____ you _____ to the supermarket? (go)

   B Yes, but we _____ a lot. (not buy)

6 A _____ you busy yesterday? (be)

   B Yes, I _____ all day. (work)

B [PAIR WORK] Talk to a partner. Ask and answer <u>five</u> questions about things you did this month. Use the questions above, or your own ideas.

C Complete the paragraph. Use simple past forms of the verbs in parentheses ( ).

At the airport, I ¹ _____ (go) to a store, and I ² _____ (buy) a cup of coffee and a sandwich. I ³ _____ (drink) the coffee, but I didn't have time to eat the sandwich. So I ⁴ _____ (take) it on the plane, and I ⁵ _____ (eat) it on the flight. I ⁶ _____ (have) lunch over the Atlantic Ocean. It was cool!

D Write about a meal you had this month. Say when and where you had it, and what you ate.

3 SPEAKING

A [PAIR WORK] Talk about a day out or trip you went on.

> On Saturday, I went out with some friends. We took a walk.

B Write <u>three</u> sentences about your day out or trip. Compare with a partner. Were your days the same or different?

> Where did you go?

4 FUNCTIONAL LANGUAGE

A   Complete the conversation with the words in the box.

| can't | don't | have | idea | Let | Let's | maybe | sorry | sure | think |

Min-jun   Why ¹ _____ we go out on Friday night?

Jamie   Um … I'm ² _____ , but I ³ _____ . I ⁴ _____ to help my father on Friday.

Min-jun   What about Saturday night?

Jamie   ⁵ _____ me think. Yes, sure. Saturday's fine.

Min-jun   OK. ⁶ _____ meet at Calendar Café. Do you know it?

Jamie   I'm not ⁷ _____ . Is it on Fourth Avenue?

Min-jun   Yes. Near the movie theater.

Jamie   OK, great. What time?

Min-jun   The café is busy on Saturday night, I ⁸ _____ . Let's get there early. How about 6 o'clock?

Jamie   Good ⁹ _____ . Then ¹⁰ _____ we can go to a movie after dinner.

B   Read the conversation and circle the correct words.

Yuri   I ¹ *really / so* like this lamb.

Susan   Thanks. Would you ² *want / like* some more?

Yuri   ³ *Yes, / No,* please. ⁴ *Can / Would* I have some more green beans, too?

Susan   ⁵ *A / Of* course. ⁶ *Here / Have* you are. Oh, please ⁷ *pass / give* the potatoes, Yuri.

Yuri   All ⁸ *course / right*. Here.

5 SPEAKING

A   PAIR WORK   Choose **one** of the situations below. Talk to a partner. Have a conversation.

1   You and your friend want to go out this weekend. Make suggestions about what you can do and where / what time you can meet. Look at page 102 for useful language.

> Let's go out on Saturday night.

2   A friend asks you about a movie. He/She wants to know the names of the actors in the movie, their nationalities, and other movies they are in. You are not 100% sure. Look at page 112 for useful language.

> Who was in *The Matrix*?

> The first Matrix movie? I'm not sure. He's American, I think. Um …

3   A friend is at your home for dinner. Offer him/her things to eat and drink. Look at page 122 for useful language.

> Would you like some chicken?

B   PAIR WORK   Change roles and have another conversation.

GRAMMAR REFERENCE AND PRACTICE

7.1 PRESENT CONTINUOUS STATEMENTS (page 67)

Present continuous statements		
	Affirmative	**Negative**
I	**'m cooking** breakfast right now.	**'m not cooking** breakfast right now.
He / She / It	**'s helping** the children. **'s taking** a shower. **'s drinking** milk.	**'s not helping** the children. **'s not taking** a shower. **'s not drinking** milk. (the cat)
You / We / They	**'re eating** breakfast. **'re cleaning** the kitchen. **'re learning** a lot at school.	**'re not eating** breakfast. **'re not cleaning** the kitchen. **'re not learning** a lot at school.

A **Put the words in the correct order to make sentences.**

1 My / aren't / TV. / parents / watching

2 coffee. / cup / drinking / a / I'm / of

3 a / She's / now. / bath / taking / right

4 TV / in / room. / Jack / his / watching / is

5 eating / the moment. / They're / breakfast / at

6 isn't / homework. / her / Maria / doing

7 our / helping / We're / now. / grandparents

7.2 PRESENT CONTINUOUS QUESTIONS (page 69)

Present continuous: *yes/no* questions and short answers		
I	**Am** I **talking** to John?	Yes, you **are**. / No, you**'re not**.
He / She / It	**Is** she **cleaning** the house? **Is** he **riding** his bike right now? **Is** it **working** at the moment?	Yes, she **is**. / No, she**'s not**. Yes, he **is**. / No, he**'s not**. Yes, it **is**. / No, it**'s not**.
You / They	**Are** you and your sister **sending** text messages? **Are** they **waiting** at the bus stop?	Yes, we **are**. / No, we**'re not**. Yes, they **are**. / No, they**'re not**.

Present continuous: information questions				
I	**Who**	**am**	I	**talking** to?
He / She / It	**Why** **Where** **How**	**is** **is** **is**	he / she he / she it	**carrying** a bag? **working** today? **going**?
You / We / They	**What** **Who**	**are** **are**	we / you / they	**doing** right now? **waiting** for?

 You can answer *Why* questions with *because*.

Why is he carrying a bag?
He's carrying a bag **because** *he has a lot of books.* (= a complete sentence)
Because *he has a lot of books.* (= an incomplete sentence in informal speech)

A **Write questions for the answers. Use the words in parentheses ( ).**

1 A _____ (you / send / a text to Carol)

   B No, I'm not. I'm calling her.

2 A _____ (why / we / wait / for Paul)

   B Because he's driving us home.

3 A _____ (Denny and Pam / do / the dishes)

   B Yes, they are.

4 A _____ (Sandra / wash / the dog)

   B No, she isn't. She's watching TV.

5 A _____ (who / your sister / help / right now)

   B My brother.

8.1 *CAN* AND *CAN'T* FOR ABILITY; *WELL* (page 77)

can and can't for ability; *well*				
	Affirmative	**Negative**	**Questions**	**Short answers**
I	**can** paint.	**can't** paint well.	**Can** I dance?	Yes, I **can** No, I **can't.**
He / She / It	**can** paint.	**can't** paint.	**Can** she dance well?	Yes, she **can.** No, she **can't.**
You / We / They	**can** paint well.	**can't** paint.	**Can** they dance?	Yes, they **can.** No, they **can't.**

A **Put the words in order to make sentences.**

1 can / well. / swim / Cathy   _____

2 a / you / car? / drive / Can   _____

3 play / I / guitar. / can't / the   _____

4 and paint? / you / Can / draw   _____

5 well. / can't / I / very / skateboard   _____

6 fix / My / table. / brother / your / can   _____

7 surf / can't / or snowboard. / I   _____

8 well. / son / can / Their / sing   _____

8.2 *CAN* AND *CAN'T* FOR POSSIBILITY (page 79)

can and can't for possibility		
Information questions with *can*		
I	**What can** I eat?	**How can** I pay for the food?
He / She /It	**Where can** he eat?	**How can** he get to the restaurant?
You / We / They	**When can** we eat?	**Who can** we have lunch with today?

A **Read the answers. Then write questions.**

1 A Where can we work?
   B We can work in the meeting room.

2 A _____ ?
   B We can watch a movie.

3 A _____ ?
   B We can get to the mall by bus.

4 A _____ ?
   B We can have a meeting on Friday.

5 A _____ ?
   B We can call my cousin.

6 A _____ ?
   B We can play basketball.

7 A _____ ?
   B We can meet at the hotel.

8 A _____ ?
   B We can take a picture with my phone.

9.1 *THIS* AND *THESE* (page 87)

This and these	
This is my ticket.	**These** are new boats.
This hotel is cheap.	**These** birds are funny.
Ryan loves **this** farm.	I don't like **these** pictures.

A **Put the words in order to make sentences.**

1 a / is / tour / This / boring.

2 these / I / birds. / like

3 sisters. / are / These / my

4 video. / watching / I'm / this

5 really / animals are / funny. / These

6 isn't / expensive. / This / vacation

9.2 *LIKE TO, WANT TO, NEED TO, HAVE TO* (page 89)

like to, want to		need to, have to	
I	**like to play** soccer. **want to play** soccer.	I	**need to work** on Saturday. **have to work** on Saturday.
He / She / It	**likes to play** soccer. **wants to play** soccer.	He / She / It	**needs to work** on Saturday **has to work** on Saturday.
You / We / They	**want to play** soccer. **like to play** soccer.	You / We / They	**need to work** on Saturday. **have to work** on Saturday.

A   **Complete the sentences with *like to, want to,* or *have to/need to* and the verbs in parentheses ( ).**

> ! You can use *need to* + a verb OR *have to* + a verb to talk about things that are necessary.

1   I _____ (swim) in the ocean, but only in July and August.

2   One day, I _____ (go) to Japan on vacation.

3   My son can't do his homework. I _____ (help) him.

4   I'm late for work, so I _____ (leave) now.

5   This is a great song. I _____ (buy) it.

6   In Japan, you _____ (drive) on the left side of the road.

7   At a movie theater, you _____ (pay) before you watch the movie.

10.1 STATEMENTS WITH *BE GOING TO* (page 99)

Statements with *be going to*		
	Affirmative	**Negative**
I	**'m going to be** home tomorrow.	**'m not going to be** home tomorrow.
He / She / It	**'s going to take** a walk in the park. **'s going to be** warm tomorrow.	**'s not going to go** shopping next week. **isn't going to be** warm tomorrow.
You / We / They	**'re going to be** here next weekend.	**'re not going to be** here next weekend.
Future time expressions		
this evening, tonight, tomorrow	on/next/this Monday	
this week/weekend/month/year	next week/weekend/month/year	

A   **Write sentences with the correct form of *be going to*.**

1   We / not play / soccer this weekend

   We're not going to play soccer this weekend   .

2   Vicky / meet / her friends tomorrow

   _____ .

3   You / have / a party for your birthday

   _____ .

4   They / not go / surf / next Saturday

   _____ .

5   I / go / dancing this evening

   _____ .

6   He / not do / the dishes after dinner

   _____ .

10.2 QUESTIONS WITH *BE GOING TO* (page 101)

be going to: yes/no questions			be going to: information questions
	yes/no questions	**Short answers**	**When are** you **going to leave?**
I	**Am I going to meet** him at 4:00?	Yes, you **are.** No, you**'re not.**	**Where is** Sofia **going to go?**
He / She / It	**Is** she **going to see** a friend?	Yes, she **is.** No, she**'s not.**	**What are** we **going to do** today? **What time is** he **going to have** lunch?
You / We / They	**Are** you **going to take** a hat?	Yes, I **am.** / Yes, we **are.** No, I**'m not.** / No, we**'re not.**	**Who are** they **going to meet?** **How are** you **going to get** to the airport?

A (Circle) the correct words to complete the sentences.

1 Are you going *buying / to buy* some new jeans?

2 Who is he going to *go / going* shopping with?

3 Is she going to *cook / cooks* dinner for four people tonight?

4 *What / What time* are we going to drive to the airport?

5 Are *your parents / Mariana* going to send him an email?

6 What *they are / are they* going to wear to the party?

11.1 STATEMENTS WITH *WAS* AND *WERE* (page 109)

Statements with *was* and *were*		
	Affirmative	**Negative**
I / He / She / It	**was** in the house.	**wasn't** noisy.
You / We / They	**were** at work.	**weren't** there.

A Complete the posts with the affirmative or negative form of *was* or *were*.

Carlene Rauss I remember a great vacation. It ¹_____ January 2010, and we
²_____ in Argentina. It ³_____ summer, so the weather ⁴_____
great! Buenos Aires is an exciting city, so we ⁵_____ really happy there. #flashbackfriday
#2010 #vacation

Paulo Soto I remember my twentieth birthday. My friends and I ⁶_____ at the
beach, but the weather ⁷_____ awful! It ⁸_____ really rainy. The café on
the beach ⁹_____ open, so there was no food. It's not a good memory because we
¹⁰_____ very happy. I mean, it ¹¹_____ a happy birthday. 😞

👍 9 🤍 4

11.2 QUESTIONS WITH *WAS* AND *WERE* (page 111)

Questions with *was* and *were*		
	yes/no questions	**Short answers**
I / He / She	**Was** she at home on Saturday?	Yes, she **was**. / No, she **wasn't**.
You / We / They	**Were** you at home on Saturday?	Yes, I **was**. / No, I **wasn't**.
Information questions with *was* and *were*		
I / He / She	**Where was** he?	
You / We / They	**How old were** you in this photo?	

A   Write questions in the simple past to match the answers.

1 _____ ?   The walls in my bedroom were blue.

2 _____ ?   My last vacation was in Brazil.

3 _____ ?   My brother's birthday party was on Friday.

4 _____ ?   Yes, my parents were at the party.

5 _____ ?   No, my house was small.

6 _____ ?   I was at work on Saturday because I was really busy.

12.1 SIMPLE PAST STATEMENTS (page 119)

Simple past statements
Use the simple past to talk about events that are in the past and finished.
I **ate** a big lunch yesterday.   We **played** soccer last weekend.   We **went** to La Paz last year.
Simple past verbs can be regular or irregular. Simple past regular verbs end in *-ed*.

Some regular verbs				
	-ed	*-d*	**double consonant + *ed***	**change *-y* to *-ied***
I / You / He / She / We / They	work**ed** play**ed** watch**ed** want**ed** walk**ed**	like**d** love**d** arrive**d** use**d** dance**d**	stop → stop**ped** chat → chat**ted**	try → tr**ied** carry → carr**ied** study → stud**ied**

Some irregular verbs					
Base form	**Simple past**	**Base form**	**Simple past**	**Base form**	**Simple past**
have	had	write	wrote	ride	rode
go	went	send	sent	fly	flew
eat	ate	buy	bought	get up	got up
drink	drank	think	thought	leave	left
do	did	run	ran	meet	met
take	took	swim	swam	sing	sang
read	read	drive	drove		

A **Complete the chart with the words in the box.**

~~arrive~~ buy drink eat go have
like need stay stop take try

Base form	Rule	Simple past
arrive	Add -*d*.	*arrived*
	Add -*ed*.	
	Double *p* and add -*ed*.	
	Change -*y* to -*ied*.	

Base form	Irregular simple past form

12.2 SIMPLE PAST QUESTIONS; *ANY* (page 121)

Simple past questions	
yes/no questions	Short answers
Did you **have** apple juice?	Yes, I/we **did**. No, I/we **didn't**.
Did we **arrive** on time?	Yes, we/you **did**. No, we/you **didn't**
Did she/he **like** the fish?	Yes, she/he **did**. No, she/he **didn't**.
Did they **go out** for dinner?	Yes, they **did**. No, they **didn't**.

Information questions		
How did	I / you	**hear** about the restaurant?
What did	you / he / she	**have** for dinner last night?
Who did	we / they	**see** at the party?

any
You can use *any* in *yes/no* questions and negative statements. *Any* = one, some, or all of something. *Not* + *any* = none.
Use *some* in affirmative statements. You can use *any* and *some* with count and non-count nouns.

Simple past questions and statements with *any*	
yes/no questions	Negative statements
Did you have **any** vegetables?	I didn't have **any** juice.
Did Mary buy **any** milk?	Joel didn't eat **any** eggs.
Did they have **any** dessert?	We didn't drink **any** soda.

A **Put the words in the correct order to make sentences.**

1 for dinner? / chicken / Did / make / you _____

2 they / did / for lunch? / have / What _____

3 eat / Did / any / vegetables? / Tonya _____

4 last night? / Where / she / go / did _____

5 coffee / buy / We / at the store. / didn't / any _____

6 at Pete's Pizza / last year? / you / Did / work _____

VOCABULARY PRACTICE

7.1 ACTIVITIES AROUND THE HOUSE (page 66)

A **Match 1–6 with a–f to complete the sentences.**

1	Do they cook ___	a	her daughter's hair.
2	Karen usually washes ___	b	your room on the weekend?
3	I do a lot of ___	c	breakfast every morning?
4	They're nice. They help ___	d	me with my English.
5	He takes ___	e	homework every day.
6	Do you clean ___	f	a shower in the evening.

B **Add the words in parentheses ( ) to the correct place in each sentence. Then write the sentences.**

1 Do you the dishes after lunch? (do)   _Do you do the dishes after lunch?_____

2 Rudy his car on the weekend. (drives)   _____

3 Does he his teeth every day? (brush)   _____

4 My mother usually cooks at 6:30. (dinner)   _____

5 She takes a every evening. (bath)   _____

6 I often my grandmother. (help)   _____

7.2 TRANSPORTATION (page 68)

A **Complete the sentences with the correct verbs in the box.**

driving	going	riding	taking	waiting	walking

1 I'm not _____ to work because my son has my car today.

2 Where are you? Mike is _____ for you at the train station.

3 Carolina is _____ with her dog in the park right now.

4 We're _____ to the mall because we need new shoes.

5 Tonya is _____ her bike to the store.

6 Mark isn't _____ the bus to class because it's late.

B **Circle the correct words to complete the sentences.**

1 Vic is at *the bus stop / his bike*.

2 Why are you carrying *a plant / the train*?

3 I usually take *the train station / the subway* to work.

4 When are you going to your *parents' house / mall*?

5 I'm sorry. I'm busy. I'm on *the bus stop / the train*.

8.1 VERBS TO DESCRIBE SKILLS (page 76)

A **Complete the sentences with the verbs in the box. You won't use all the verbs.**

dance	fix	play	skateboard	speak
draw	paint	sing	snowboard	swim

1 I don't _____. There's a mountain near me but it doesn't have snow on it.

2 My friends usually _____ the guitar and _____ songs after dinner.

3 In my art class, we _____ and _____ a lot of different things.

4 I _____ two languages – English and Korean.

5 In February and March, I _____ in the ocean.

6 Do you have a problem with your laptop? My brothers _____ computers.

B **Complete the words with vowels (a, e, i, o, u).**

1 d _a_ nc _e_

2 f ___ x th___ ngs

3 sn___ wb___ ___ rd

4 sw___ m

5 pl___ y the g___ ___ t___ r

6 sp___ ___ k tw___ l___ ng___ ___ g___ s

7 r___ ___ d m___ s___ c

8 dr___ w

9 sk___ t___ b___ ___ rd

10 p___ ___ nt

11 s___ ng

12 s___ rf

8.2 WORK (page 78)

A Complete the sentences with the words in the box.

break	coworkers	have	think
company	hard	office	worker

1 I work for a big American _____ .

2 I have a new desk and a chair in my _____ .

3 She's doing a great job. She's a very good _____ .

4 It's time to take a _____ and have a cup of coffee.

5 I work in a team with six _____ .

6 We're always busy. We work _____ .

7 Can we talk about this? Can we _____ a meeting?

8 I don't know the answer. Can I _____ about it for five minutes?

B Circle the word that doesn't belong in each group.

1 living room   office   kitchen   bedroom

2 have a meeting   play games   call a coworker   work hard

3 drink coffee   have lunch   take a break   have a meeting

4 company   couch   chair   desk

5 worker   brother   teacher   coworker

9.1 TRAVEL (page 86)

A Circle the correct words to complete the sentences.

1 I have a *ticket / tour* for the bus.

2 This *city / ranch* is in the country.

3 I'm on *vacation / country* with my family.

4 My seat on the *plane / ticket* is by the window.

5 My house is in a small *town / boat*, but I work in the city.

6 This *tour / ticket* is expensive, but it's really interesting.

B Circle the word that doesn't belong in each group.

1 vacation   tour   work

2 ranch   farm   ticket   country

3 boat   hotel   plane   bus

4 ticket   tour   plane   friend

5 country   town   city

9.2 TRAVEL ARRANGEMENTS (page 88)

A **Match 1–6 with a–f to complete the sentences.**

1 You can buy tickets ___
2 We can check in for our ___
3 I don't usually travel on ___
4 We're arriving at our ___
5 I'm staying at a really nice ___
6 We're flying from the new ___

a destination.
b airport.
c online.
d trains.
e flight.
f hotel.

B **David is traveling from Chicago to London. Put his trip in the correct order.**

_g_ → ___ → ___ → ___ → ___ → ___ → ___ → ___

a Stay in the hotel.
b Drive to the airport.
c Arrive at the hotel.
d Leave home.

e Take a bus from the airport to the hotel.
f Check in for the flight at the airport.
g Buy a plane ticket online.
h Fly to the destination.

10.1 GOING OUT (page 98)

A (Circle) **the correct word to complete the sentences.**

1 Can you *meet / go* me at the airport on Friday?
2 Jennifer wants to *take / look* her brother to lunch for his birthday.
3 We're *doing / having* a picnic right now.

4 I like to *get / meet* together with friends on the weekends.
5 Do you usually *make / go* shopping at the mall?
6 I never *take / eat* outside.

B **Complete the sentences with the words in the box.**

> art   coffee   family   hotel   shopping   walk

1 Do you want to take a _____ in the park?
2 I like to look at interesting _____ in museums.
3 I want to take you out for _____ to my favorite café.
4 We often get together with _____ on the weekends.
5 I have to meet my coworker at his _____ on Friday.
6 Maria never goes _____ with us. She doesn't like it.

10.2 CLOTHES; SEASONS (page 100)

A **Complete the clothes words with vowels (*a, e, i, o, u*).**

1 I want to buy some j___ ___ns and a sw___ ___t___r.
2 I'm going to wear a T-sh___rt and sh___rts to the beach.
3 This store sells sh___ ___s and b___ ___ts.

4 I'm going to buy a winter c___ ___t and h___t.
5 We usually wear p___nts and a sh___rt at work.
6 Is she going to wear a dr___ss or a sk___rt?

B **Complete the paragraph with the words in the box.**

dry season	fall	rainy season	spring	summer	winter

In Japan, we have four seasons. I love ¹_____ and ²_____ because there are a lot of flowers then. After summer, it's ³_____ , and this is usually from September to November. Then it's ⁴_____ , and you can do a lot of fun activities, for example, snowboard in the mountains. We have a short ⁵_____ , too. It usually starts in June and ends in July, and it is *very* rainy. We don't have a ⁶_____ in Japan. It's not a desert country.

11.1 DESCRIBING PEOPLE, PLACES, AND THINGS (page 108)

A **Match the sentences with the correct responses.**

1 This new restaurant isn't good. ___
2 Your daughter is quiet. ___
3 This is a beautiful picture. ___
4 I love beach parties. ___
5 The train was very slow today. ___
6 These children are really noisy. ___

a Thanks. I think the artist is wonderful.
b Really? It's usually fast.
c Yes, but they're really cute.
d That's true. She's really shy.
e I know. The food is awful.
f Me, too. They're exciting, and the ocean is beautiful.

B **Read the sentences and complete the words.**

1 My cousin is **b**_____ , and her children are really **c**_____ .
2 It's a nice, **q**_____ restaurant, and it has **w**_____ food!
3 This movie is **a**_____ . It's **s**_____ and boring.
4 I love soccer games. They're always **n**_____ and **e**_____ .
5 My brother's happy because he has a **n**_____ car.
   It's really **f**_____ .

11.2 COLORS (page 110)

A **Unscramble the color words (1–10.) Then match the words to the colors (a–j).**

1 dre _____
2 nreeg _____
3 leub _____
4 tiwhe _____
5 weyoll _____
6 nbwor _____
7 knip _____
8 ragnoe _____
9 ygre _____
10 klacb _____

a ● ___
b ● ___
c ● ___
d ● ___
e ● ___
f ● ___
g ● ___
h ● ___
i ○ ___
j ● ___

B **Match five of the colors in exercise A to the things below.**

1 some milk _____
2 a coffee with milk _____
3 some grass _____
4 the ocean _____
5 an elephant _____

12.1 SNACKS AND SMALL MEALS (page 118)

A   **Look at the pictures. Write the words in the chart.**

Fruit and vegetables	Meat	Dairy products	Grains	Small meals

B   (Circle) **the correct words to complete the sentences.**

1 **A** What do you want with your crackers?

    B I want cheese and *tomatoes / coconut*, please.

2 For a small meal, I like soup and *bread / potato*.

3 My favorite sandwich has bread, *butter / orange*, and chicken.

4 Beef is very good with *bananas / tomatoes*.

5 My brother really likes fruit. He eats bananas and *apples / lamb* every day.

12.2 MORE FOOD, DRINKS, AND DESSERTS (page 120)

A   **Complete the menu with the words in the box.**

beans	chocolate cake	cookies	ice cream
juice	pizza	soda	

B   (Circle) **the correct words to complete the sentences.**

1 *Steak / Rice* is my favorite meat.

2 *Cookies / Green beans* are good for you because they are vegetables.

3 Do you want some *pizza / ice cream* for dessert?

4 I like to eat *eggs / water* for breakfast.

5 Did you drink any *rice / juice* with your meal?

6 *Chocolate cake / soda* is my favorite dessert.

—— Meals ——
Fish with rice and black
1 _____

Cheese and tomato
2 _____

—— Drinks ——
3 _____
Apple, orange, or pineapple
4 _____

—— Desserts ——
5 _____
6 _____
7 _____

PROGRESS CHECK

Can you do these things? Check (✓) what you can do. Then write your answers in your notebook.

UNIT 7

Now I can …	Prove it
☐ use words about activities around the house.	Write three things you do around the house.
☐ use the present continuous.	Write a sentence about what you are doing right now. Write a sentence about what your teacher is doing.
☐ use transportation words.	Complete the sentences with transportation words. *I'm on the _____ right now. Are you _____ to work? We're riding our _____ to the park.*
☐ ask *yes/no* and information questions in the present continuous.	Write one *yes/no* question and two information questions. Use the present continuous.
☐ start a phone call.	Write a way to answer the phone. Write a question to ask people how they are.
☐ write a blog about things happening now.	Read your blog from lesson 7.4. Find a way to improve it. Use the Accuracy check, Register check, and the new language from this unit.

UNIT 8

Now I can …	Prove it
☐ talk about skills.	Write five skills that your friends or people in your family have. Use *can*.
☐ use *can* to talk about ability.	Write a sentence about something you can do well and a sentence about something you can't do well.
☐ talk about work.	Write three things that people do at work.
☐ use *can* to talk about possibility.	Write two questions. Use *What … ?* and *Where … ? + can*.
☐ give opinions.	Do you think technology is good for the world? Write a short answer.
☐ write an online comment.	Read your online comment from lesson 8.4. Find a way to improve it. Use the Accuracy check, Register check, and the new language from this unit.

UNIT 9

Now I can …	Prove it
☐ use travel words.	Where can you take a tour? What do you need a ticket for? Answer the questions about your city or country.
☐ use *this* and *these*.	Complete these sentences with your own ideas. *I _____ this _____.* *I _____ these _____.*
☐ talk about travel arrangements.	Think of a city in your country, or in another country. Describe the trip from your home to the city.
☐ use *like to, want to, have to, need to*.	Write four sentences about things you like to do, want to do, have to do, and need to do.
☐ ask for information in a store.	Write three questions to ask for missing information. Begin your questions with *Where … ?, How much … ?*, and *What time does … ?* Then write the answers to your questions.
☐ write a description of a place.	Read your description of a place from lesson 9.4. Find a way to improve it. Use the Accuracy check, Register check, and the new language from this unit.

PROGRESS CHECK

Can you do these things? Check (✓) what you can do. Then write your answers in your notebook.

Now I can …	Prove it	UNIT 10
☐ use words for going out activities.	How many going out activities can you remember? Make a list.	
☐ use *be going to* in statements.	Write two sentences about what you're going to do next month. Write two sentences about what you're <u>not</u> going to do next year.	
☐ use words for clothes and seasons.	What's your favorite season? What do you usually wear to class? What do you wear when you go out with your friends?	
☐ ask *yes/no* and information questions with *be going to*.	Complete these questions. Then write answers for you. *Are* _____ *(you, work) this summer? What* _____ *(you, do) for your next birthday?*	
☐ make and respond to suggestions.	Complete the suggestions with *Why don't we* or *Let's*. Then write answers to the suggestions. _____ *meet at a café tomorrow.* _____ *go shopping after class?*	
☐ write an online invitation.	Read your online invitation from lesson 10.4. Find a way to improve it. Use the Accuracy check, Register check, and the new language from this unit.	

Now I can …	Prove it	UNIT 11
☐ use adjectives to describe people, places, and things.	Write three sentences. Use adjectives to describe a person, a place, and a thing.	
☐ use *was* and *were* in statements.	Write four sentences about the past. Use *was*, *were*, *wasn't*, and *weren't*.	
☐ talk about colors.	Look around you. What things can you see? What color are they? Write five sentences.	
☐ ask questions with *was* and *were*.	Write two questions with *was* and two questions with *were*.	
☐ express uncertainty.	Write the capital city of these countries: Australia, Germany, India, Indonesia. In your answer, write that you're not sure.	
☐ write an email about things you keep from the past.	Read your email from lesson 11.4. Find a way to improve it. Use the Accuracy check, Register check, and the new language from this unit.	

Now I can …	Prove it	UNIT 12
☐ talk about snacks and small meals.	Write about food you like and don't like. Write about five things.	
☐ use simple past statements.	Write four sentences about things you did yesterday.	
☐ talk about food, drinks, and desserts.	Write something you ate yesterday, or last week, for dessert. Write something you drank.	
☐ use simple past questions.	Write three questions to ask a partner about what he or she did last week.	
☐ offer and request food and drink.	Imagine you're in a restaurant. Write a question the server asks, and write your answer.	
☐ write a restaurant review.	Read your restaurant review from lesson 12.4. Find a way to improve it. Use the Accuracy check, Register check, and the new language from this unit.	

PAIR WORK PRACTICE (STUDENT A)

7.3 EXERCISE 2D STUDENT A

Imagine you're talking to your partner on the phone. Say the news below, and your partner reacts. Then your partner says some news to you, and you react. Take turns.

1 My new job is really boring.
2 I'm having a cup of coffee.
3 It's my birthday today.
4 My dog is eating my lunch.
5 The people at my new college are friendly.
6 I'm on the subway.

8.3 EXERCISE 2D STUDENT A

1 Say the sentences below to your partner. Add information to explain or say more. Then your partner gives his or her opinion.

- Basketball is/isn't my favorite sport. I mean, …
- I can/can't read music. It's difficult/easy. I mean, …
- I like / don't like art. I mean, …
- I think computer skills are important. I mean, …

> Basketball is my favorite sport. I mean, I can play really well, and it's fun.

> I don't like basketball. I think soccer is the best sport.

2 Listen to your partner. Then give your opinion.

10.3 EXERCISE 2D STUDENT A

Your partner makes a suggestion. You say you can't and give a reason. Take turns.

Suggestion	Reason
have coffee now	(Your partner)
(Your partner)	go home at lunchtime
have a meeting on Monday	(Your partner)
(Your partner)	go to the supermarket
go shopping on Saturday	(Your partner)
(Your partner)	work late

> Let's have coffee now.

> I'm sorry, but I can't. I have to go to a meeting.

11.3 EXERCISE 2D STUDENT A

1 Ask your partner these questions. Listen to their answers. Then tell your partner the correct answers.

Question	Answer
What was Leonardo DiCaprio's name in *Titanic*?	Jack Dawson
Where is the singer Carol Konka from?	Brazil
What country is *Crouching Tiger Hidden Dragon* from?	China
What was Elvis's last name?	Presley
What band is Chris Martin in?	Coldplay
What was the dog's name in *The Wizard of Oz*?	Toto

> What was Leonardo DiCaprio's name in *Titanic*?

> Uh, I think it was Jack. / Um, I have no idea.

> It was Jack Dawson.

2 Answer your partner's questions. Use expressions of uncertainty for answers you don't know or are unsure about.

This page is intentionally left blank

PAIR WORK PRACTICE (STUDENT B)

7.3 EXERCISE 2D   STUDENT B

Imagine you're talking to your partner on the phone. Your partner says some news to you, and you react. Then you say the news below, and your partner reacts. Take turns.

1 I'm cooking dinner.
2 I'm at a party on the beach.
3 I'm watching TV.

4 I'm working on Saturday and Sunday.
5 I have a new plane.
6 My train is three hours late.

8.3 EXERCISE 2D   STUDENT B

1 **Listen to your partner. Then give your opinion.**

> Basketball is my favorite sport. I mean, I can play really well, and it's fun.

> I don't like basketball. I think soccer is the best sport.

2 **Say the sentences to your partner. Add information to explain or say more. Then your partner gives his or her opinion.**

- Friday is/isn't my favorite day. I mean, …
- I like / don't like music. I mean, …
- I can/can't snowboard. It's difficult/easy. I mean, …
- I think good food is important. I mean, …

10.3 EXERCISE 2D   STUDENT B

You make a suggestion. Your partner says he/she can't and gives a reason. Take turns.

Suggestion	Reason for refusal
(Your partner)	go to a meeting
have lunch	(Your partner)
(Your partner)	go out
take a walk after work	(Your partner)
(Your partner)	study this weekend
watch a movie tonight	(Your partner)

> Let's have coffee now.

> I'm sorry, but I can't. I have to go to a meeting.

11.3 EXERCISE 2D   STUDENT B

1 **Answer your partner's questions. Use expressions of uncertainty for answers you don't know or are unsure.**

2 **Ask your partner these questions. Listen to their answers. Then tell your partner the correct answers.**

Question	Answer
What was Kate Winslet's name in *Titanic*?	Rose
Where is the band *Awesome City Club* from?	Japan
How many *Pirates of the Caribbean* movies was Johnny Depp in?	five
What is Shakira's last name?	Mebarak Ripoll
What band was John Lennon in?	The Beatles
What animals are in *101 Dalmatians*?	dogs

> What was Leonardo DiCaprio's name in *Titanic*?

> Uh, I think it was Jack. / Um, I have no idea.

> It was Jack Dawson.